PERSEUS
IN THE WIND

FREYA STARK

CENTURY PUBLISHING

LONDON

To

JOHN AND SKIMPER

First published in Great Britain in 1948 by
John Murray

This edition published 1984 by
Century Publishing Co. Ltd
Portland House,
12–13 Greek Street,
London WIV 5LE

Wood Engravings by Reynolds Stone

ISBN 0 7126 0363 8

Cover shows a painting from the
collection at the Mathaf Gallery,
24 Motcomb Street, London.

Printed in Great Britain by
Richard Clay (The Chaucer Press) Ltd, Bungay, Suffolk

CONTENTS

Those earthly godfathers of heaven's lights
That give a name to every fixèd star,
Have no more profit of their shining nights
Than those that walk and wot not what they are.

Love's Labour Lost.

Oh no! it is an ever-fixèd mark
That looks on tempests, and is never shaken:
It is the star to every wandering bark,
Whose worth's unknown although his height be taken.

SHAKESPEARE. Sonnet.

FOREWORD

ONE summer I spent some weeks in Persia among the mountains of Elburz, and rode or walked about the passes that separate the Caspian jungle from the plain of Qazvin. I still think of these landscapes as among the most beautiful in the world, and remember long days on stony paths, with the bells of the mules tinkling behind me as they found their steps in valleys yet unmapped, by rarely visited streams.

The villages lie north and south of the main range on cultivated slopes in the sun's eye, by the banks of waters shaded under trees. They have little to do with the southern plain whose wall is notched in their skyline, where a few steep ways lead down; but within the mountain cradles one valley communicates freely with another by routes of boulders worn through centuries of traffic, that wind in loops and zigzags over watersheds. From the edges of the snow one looks back, and sees the villages by their waters like dull brown beads strung on the light thread of the track; they become smaller and smaller, until the thread continues alone and reaches the pass, and ties with loose and twisted ends on to another thread, that drops to another necklace of villages by another stream, upon the farther side.

The mountains are high, and uninhabited stretches separate the last and smallest village from the first one on the other watershed; the track to the pass climbs among rocks with glistening scales of mica in waterless ravines; the trees that follow some vein of moisture die away in stunted growths of thorn until there is only juniper flattened by wind among boulders; and this, too, gives way at last to the short grass that grows in the pockets of the snow. Then one may taste the northern wind and know that the pass is near.

Some of these crossings are difficult and lonely, and one can walk a day without meeting a traveller; but others are highways in a land where wheeled traffic is unknown; and all morning long the caravans go up or down, and the bells of the mules and the songs of the Charvadars and the thwack of their sticks on the obstinate buttocks of their animals resound and echo, and make a liveliness among the naked hills. The traffic has regular hours, determined by the distance of villages with stabling for the night. Usually, as the afternoon declines, human voices cease; some shepherd will talk or pipe to his flock from a rock where pastures end; apart from him the eagles fly alone. With the coming of night the babble of the streams rises from all their valleys, not loud but clear because of the silence of the waterless places where the smooth winds are heard as they move from shoulder to shoulder.

Then the pass becomes a gateway to the stars.

Beyond a black saddle, between buttresses whose detail is lost or wanly shining perhaps with snow, the stars hang as if the edge of the world were there and one could reach them. They swing in the night-wind that makes them twinkle and never touches earth; and their shivering light, and their steadfast journeying and their repeated presence make them companions as one lies sheltered in some corrie, a part of the shadow of the hills.

It happened that in this Elburz summer the constellation of *Perseus* night after night spanned the gap of the pass with his scimitar. He danced in a wind whose earthly brother blew thin from the north and the Caspian Sea. I came to feel his stars as a friendliness and a bond in the gaiety of spaces and the cold of night. The memory has remained and has given the name of *Perseus* to this book, in which I have written about things that are beyond our grasp yet visible to all, dear to our hearts and far from our understanding as the constellations; a comfort for the frail light they shed. Without being astronomers, in our separate darkness, we rejoice in them, and from our caves, our twilights of belief and ignorant names and lonely journeys, feel that we are a fellowship that looks to the same stars.

Asolo, Summer 1947.

1

THE PAGAN GOWN

Il tenait pour innocent tout ce qui ne fait de mal à personne. Aussi avait-il dans l'âme plus de douceur que n'en permettent les lois, les moeurs and les croyances diverses des peuples.

ANATOLE FRANCE. *Le Mannequin d'Osier.*

When thou lookest upon the imperfections of others, allow one eye for what is laudable in them, and the balance they have from some excellency, which may render them considerable.

SIR THOMAS BROWNE. *Christian Morals.*

. . . to mark
the long way back that climbs for all of us
untrodden and enchanted through the dark.

HUMBERT WOLFE. *Requiem.*

L'eau qui passe pour vierge était plusieurs fois veuve.

J. COCTEAU. *Léone.*

Oh sencelesse man, who cannot possibly make a worme, and yet will make Gods by dozens.

MONTAIGNE. *Essays.* Florio's trans.

There is no soundness in them, whom aught of Thy creation displeaseth;

ST. AUGUSTINE. *Confessions.*

L'Eglise triomphante accueille, à côté des saints de profession, d'aimables pécheurs prédestinés au salut éternel. Elle gagne, à cette pratique, de mettre une agréable diversité parmi les élus.

ANATOLE FRANCE. *Vie Litt., Vol. II.*

Everyone knows that it is a coat of many colours, that is, diversified with a beautiful variety.

ST. BERNARD OF CLAIRVAUX.

1. THE PAGAN GOWN

THERE is a pleasantly pagan atmosphere about the countryside of my Italian home. Trees here and there, hornbeam or mulberry, are twisted in a canopy of boughs; and an oleograph of St. Anthony, or of the Madonna and Child, is plaited in the leafy frame. The growing shrine stands usually in a hedge or beside a gate, to guard the crops behind it; and the older peasants, moving with a slow swing and muddy boots beside their creaking oxen may be heard even to-day to mutter ejaculations to Bacchus or Diana or, possibly, in one breath, to Hercules and the Virgin together.

Who does not feel pagan in the spring? That languor, when first the grass blade is folded so that it can hold a shadow; when lakes are soft, the colour of mist and light; when the streams run transparent with liquid notes, their wavelets cold as snowdrops. Cats lie in the sun with the five toes of each paw stretched out, and sleep, like a slow serpent, moves up and down their spine. The notes of birds at evening drop like water falling in water; and the buds, especially beech, have a sharp and bitter smell. The earth is damp, sucking dead leaves down into the furnace of her year, working at growth in warmth and darkness. I hope old age will not deprive me of this repeated visitation of delight in which, with the whole of our planet, we turn ourselves in space towards the sun. While this is happening, the puritan dies in us; there is a soul in inanimate things. Our Monsignor with his little procession walks about, blessing the fields or sprinkling holy water in the houses. His choir boys follow him, with white cassocks and tidy hair, and muddy boots from the paths round their homes. They

3

carry their brass bowl and the olive bough for sprinkling with a nonchalant air, for they too are distracted by the many voices. Their ceremony is part of a ritual far older than anything our civilizations can remember; and the Church, like a great ship under sail, carries as its ballast, hidden far below the water-line, the whole pagan history of men.

One wonders when the puritan first began. This cleavage of poly- and mono-theist, of hedonist and ascetic, of Epicurean and Stoic, of Catholic and Protestant, seems to be one of the genuine divisions of human kind. What first made the creature dissatisfied with that which for all the rest of creation appears to be sufficient? Perhaps it was the desert, where "the barren earth entwines few tentacles about the heart; it stretches away dark and empty beneath our feet, a mere footstool for meditation."*

This is tiresome about the puritan. Why must things be gaunt and bare for people to meditate upon them?

Whatever the ultimate origins, the book of Genesis gives a summary of the repeated story: delight in external things, and then human hunger for truth beyond. Eve, Psyche, Pandora, they would look, not, like the Lady of Shalot, *away* from the mirror, but *through* it, to see what is hidden behind the moving show: until the face of things becomes an impediment to them and a torment, a barrier to the simplicity of truth.

One of the more charming Muhammedan saints walked always barefoot out of respect for earth, the carpet of God. Indeed the kindlier among saints have all found the same answer, seeing the divine unity in all its variegated vestments of fugitive beauty and transitory life. But ordinary sons of men quarrel to this day, unable to walk the tightrope between worship of creatures on the one hand and on the other a blindness towards the presence of what is divine. A fair protestant, I am yet inclined to think the pagan in less danger: to kiss the hem of a garment in reverence is better than to have it fluttering unrecognized about one. The windows of hill towns that shine in dawn or sunset are but paltry glass that tells of the hidden sun: yet the inexperienced eye that thinks it fire, may be pardoned

* GEORGE SANTAYANA. *Soliloquies in England*, p. 13.

for not realizing how far beyond the horizon are its origins. So, indirectly, in our everyday life we see the presence of God. The eagle-sighted alone can witness it unhooded, or those whose wings are feathered for great space. Yet the reflection is indeed originally sunlight, and if sometimes we forget the interval and distance of its journey, and worship—that is surely more venial than to forget altogether that its glitter is divine.

For this reason I have no quarrel with superstition, unless cruelty comes to darken and corrupt.

In southern India, where one lives in a happy muddle of familiarity with gods, and even the little chipmunk has a place in temples—since Rama stroked him with his fingers and left the three streaks down his back—I was surprised to find how natural paganism appears.

What else but those crowded pyramids of deity would one expect above the seething tanks whose steps are alive all day with naked limbs below the white and red-striped temple walls? Sea-waves beat the shore of this land with the strength of a bull's neck; one can feel their pull in a few inches of water, for they have the whole emptiness westward from Australia in which to gather themselves together. In the forests that clothe the mountain horizon thin-flanked flat-headed tigers roam, and cobras sway with glazed eyes in the sun. How can man, living in his coconut strip of land, in a sort of under-water atmosphere, dim green beneath the unending aisles and fronds, think of himself as more than a part of it all?

Once a year the gods leave their temples and, escorted by king, court, cabinet and army, bathe themselves in the sunset and the sea; and pass, with their elephants and drums, between the soldiers in smart uniforms of Europe who line a sanded path where all walk barefoot, attending the smiling gods borne on their stands. In the evening, after this has happened, they walk abroad. In the mute streets, in rich darkness, scented and heavy with flowers, the people come to look. Their king must shoot an arrow in their defence, and no sound warns the enemy till all is over. The enemy's head is a coconut hidden in a little hut of leaves at a crossroads; and here, under the stars, the whole town gathers; their white gowns are visible dimly; the sound of their brown feet is

5

smothered in the sand; and they wait, thousands of them, in silence.

Presently, still soundless, with torches in clusters, and shields and bows, the procession comes from the temple. The gods in their wreaths and flowers are placed to see. And, humbly, in a plain toga, with bare shoulders, a lamp and a bow in his hands, the king advances. He places the lamp on the ground and fits his arrow and, standing alone in front of the hidden malignity, shoots fair and true. So small and humble, he seems the epitome of man fighting with the courage created by the presence of his gods; and as the arrow finds its mark, the people shout, the drums and trumpets make all the noise they can; and city and temple are safe for another year.

I have watched the same sort of ceremony in the Alps, at the yearly blessing of the Monte Rosa glacier. A small procession gathers in the last village beyond Macugnaga, and walks behind the cross and the priest in yellow cope with swinging incense, across the meadows where the harvested hay and the fountains of wild roses are breathing out a summer incense of their own. The glacier pours down into the head of the valley, threatening the pastures beyond its drift of boulder-strewn moraine. At its edge the flowers have thinned away to *soldanella* or *ranunculus glacialis*; all else is only the makings of earth out of chaos, the oozing clay and sobbing patches where ice-water breaks through, and steep torrents, white and green, that swell in the afternoons with the melting snowfields, and shrink again at night.

Facing all this, on the cushiony grass of pastures, the little ceremony is performed: the cross is lifted, and the prayer spoken that is to hold the slow-moving giant in its bond; and he, overhanging with glittering height, and icy caverns and pinnacles against the burning sky, declares, with the contrast of his hugeness, the glory and audacity of man.

Religion is all an adventure in courage, and superstition a print of adventuring footsteps in the past, though it is apt to become more coercive than a footprint and to freeze, if it can, the exploring spirit from which itself was born. That, I imagine, is why the mystic is inclined to retreat from the habitations of man; to seek a world where every object he sees

6

is not wound in a cocoon of thought and images created by others. He needs to get away from all these voices, he needs a footstool for meditation, and to watch, in the silence of his own heart, for the trail which so many wayfarers have confused. The true call of the desert, of the mountains, or the sea, is their silence—free of the network of dead speech. This silence without which no enduring progress can be built must enter into all education that is worthy of the name: it is the reason why climbing or walking or sailing should come, if possible, into the life of every child:

"The thought of death sits easy on the man
Who has been born and dies among the mountains."*

Some people, out of strength or weakness, come to love such solitude as the breath of life. Many, strangers to their own souls, shun it with fear. But the well-strung creature finds in it a tonic, a pause from which he comes refreshed. With the mountain lightness still in his eyes and feet, he is happy to return from the wilderness and to find himself again among the paths and dwellings and habits, the rites and symbols which in their long trail of history have made him what he is.

* W. WORDSWORTH. *The Brothers.*

2

SERVICE

Leadership was not a mere matter of transmitting orders but of evoking the will to serve.

ARTHUR BRYANT. *Years of Victory.*

There have been men that have surpassed their fate finding a star in the mud. These in the things they could have had and left unclaimed were great these in the kingdoms they refused were kings.

HUMBERT WOLFE. *Requiem.*

Who love their fellows even to the death,
Who feel the giant agony of the world,
And more, like slaves to poor humanity,
Labour for mortal good?

KEATS. *Fall of Hyperion.*

Umile ed alta più che creatura.

DANTE. *Paradiso.*

. . . 'tis mad idolatry
To make the service greater than the god.

Troilus and Cressida.

Teachers and pupils seemed animals of different species, useful and well-disposed towards each other, like a cow and a milkmaid; periodic contributions could pass between them, but not conversation.

GEORGE SANTAYANA. *Character and Opinion in the U.S.A.*

. . . the gentle
who are as rich as the blades of grass, that stand
content to be one thread in the green mantle
in which spring enters in Broceliande.

HUMBERT WOLFE. *Requiem.*

2. SERVICE

SERVICE became the instrument not only of Christianity but of every religion in the world, long before houses or housemaids were invented. It was the rose in the first desert, and still makes life possible for nurses, government officials, men in offices, whose work might otherwise be arid beyond their capacity to bear. It endows humble people with their chance of the greatest of worldly luxuries, since it makes of their labour, which is the only commodity they have, a thing that can be given. And it is free from the dangers of philanthropy, since it is free from arrogance. Its secret of happiness is made manifest in any crisis, when men forget to care about their rights and think of service only.

It is, however, a two-sided virtue, not—like Love its begetter—a "native of the rocks" and master of men. It needs a receiver as well as a giver and thrives on some small meed of welcome and honour; it is founded on co-operation. Not so long ago, a chit was circulated through government offices, begging them to recollect that "the member of another department is not necessarily an enemy". Bureaucracy, one fears, believes in economic man and is apt, by so doing, to despise service, having forgotten not so much to give as to receive.

In spite of the Gospel, is it not hard to decide which of these two is the more blessed in a world where to accept with discrimination sums up the art of life? I am inclined to prefer the receiver. To give is pleasure and gratification: perhaps the word "blessed" had such a meaning, and our puritan background alone added the atmosphere of duty and constraint? But as to an obligation to *receive*, there can surely be no doubt about it?

When service is offered with pleasure, how boorish to take it as a right! Here is the origin of domestic trouble, and at the root of it the materialism which in the past accepted lives of men as a commodity to be bought and in the present takes them to depend on wages.

The modern world has made wages indispensable and compulsory, and who would quarrel with them for being so? Artists also, and members of Parliament are paid, yet scarcely work for hire: for that is not the beginning and end of the affair. It turns men sour to ask for bread and to be offered coin merely. And if the reformer, walking through his legislated town, turns some sudden corner and, in a byway sheltered in tranquillity, finds One bent low to wash His servants' feet —he will be much mistaken if he thinks that he can multiply this happy vision by any increase in anybody's pay. He has tried and found a poor enough response in cooks and housemaids; yet the voice from Jerusalem still calls its volunteers.

Three years ago I returned to my Italian home. It had very recently been freed from the retreating Germans and no news of it had yet come through. I flew from Rome and circled over the neighbouring Treviso and saw denuded roofs like spider webs, their skeletons exposed, their tiles in heaps around them; for a third of that little town had been damaged by bombs. An army car took me to Padua and up to the hills next day, along a road grey-green with captured transport, where no civilian traffic yet appeared. Peaceful-ness and cultivated crops lay open on either hand. Peasants were gathered in Sunday crowds on the steps of churches, swinging long round capes and wearing black sombreros that have been the fashion ever since I can remember. We drove up the hill and I saw my house standing. The arch of a forgotten gateway spans the road and a carved Renais-sance fountain is beyond, of stone worn smooth and yellow. When I rang my bell, Emma in white apron came with the gardener and my mother's secretary behind her: it was as if the years since September 1939 had vanished.

Six Fascist generals and ministers in turn inhabited my home, and its garden was scraped brown by the sentinels' feet; the furniture had been treated roughly; the laurels by the door cut down to make a "field of fire" against partisans advancing up the road. Only a week saved it, for this district was to be the last defence between Piave and Brenta, and a big German gun was already half-way up the hill: it was to be placed in my garden, but the retreat grew too swift and the Germans went. The town was still full of tremors: substantial notaries and burgesses had been hiding in garrets and cellars; one does not get over all this in a day. There were hold-ups too once a week or so, in lonely houses and villages all through that autumn and winter, and the very heart of authority was weakened; two black-masked assailants in one robbery were shot, and were found to be a local bank manager and a sergeant of carabiniers.

The stories of these events, beating like drums in a cave, made them seem greater than themselves. Every day had its toll of murder, to which people had become accustomed during the Fascist occupation, so that the scales of normal living were forgotten. There was one tale of a woman who went to the market town to sell her cow. She had been warned by her brother-in-law of the dangers of the lonely way home with so much money on her, and had taken his revolver to defend herself. When she had sold her cow and was leaving the town she met an acquaintance and told him of her brother-in-law's kindness in lending the revolver. "Why," said the man, when he looked at it, "he has given it to you without loading it. You had better take mine." So they exchanged weapons, and on the way home a man sprang out at her, and she fired and killed him. When they took off his mask, she recognized the brother-in-law who had lent the unloaded gun.

Through all this chaos the personal feelings, that private grace which in Italy makes up for the absence of so many public virtues, stood firm. When I returned, the little town looked upon me as a symbol of British friendship, gave me a welcome and offered its civic freedom. The chattels people had hidden for us at great risk were brought in processions of handcarts and barrows; and the small factory my mother fostered was found to be still alive, held together by Caroli, her pretty secretary, with no expectation of profit or reward. Through the war years it served as a secret meeting-place of partisans, whose boots and candle-ends still lay about there.

We had great difficulties during these first months. The food ration was almost entirely theoretical; the only person who never exceeded it was said to have been granted a *posthumous* reward. There was comparative plenty in the lands across the Po, and I mentioned to the Allied Military Government that, whatever the rules might be, I was going to get enough corn to feed my house and eight work girls through the winter: they told me not to fetch more than was strictly necessary and not to get caught: Caroli treated with a friendly partisan and we ferried a few sacks in a boat across the Po at night time. For clothing, we found some wool among the hidden goods of the house and every girl wove herself a warm coat in her spare time and one for Emma to end up with. I came to Italy many months ahead of any other returning resident, and of course was allowed no money by my government to live on: but a trunk that was saved was full of linen sheets and we sold these from time to time to pay the bills. While I was busy with this, Emma came to me one day and said she felt she could subtract 100 lire a month from her wages, though they were low enough according to the standard of this time. Caroli is now a partner in the factory, and has never received nor wished for any financial reward for those devoted years. It would take much from life if this luxury of giving were denied; or if kindness were not expected in return, so that one may remember that it is not the bond of wages *only* which binds us.

This relationship of service is based on an instinct so delicate and universal that it will blossom whenever a chance is given. It creates perhaps the purest of human affections, asking least and offering all. I have found it in many various places. Our Devonshire gardener followed my father to his fruit-farm in Canada and begged to stay by him without wages during two bad years when a blizzard had destroyed the trees. Among the Arabs the feeling is particularly deep and strong: in a strange house, a personal servant will wrap himself in his shawl and lie stretched across the threshold of the door to guard it; and—if allowed to do so—he will consider himself to be intended in all things so to be interposed between

14

his master and the annoyances of life. I think it is sheer laziness that has tended to destroy the bond in Britain: we are not fond as other races are of the actual wear and tear of human relationships, and it is less trouble to pay in money than to be active and grateful in the return of kindness.

But in affairs other than domestic we have not lost the knowledge; and if we built an empire better than we can now run a house it was because the edifice was founded less on dominion than on service. Wherever this has been completely so it has stood firm; and even in many places where the idol of domination has been installed, it has been saved from offence—partially or altogether—by a passion among government officials of all sorts to dedicate themselves to the people among whom they happen to be placed. This passion, the only thing that can make empires last, is looked upon with suspicion by bureaucratic blindness; yet it is service rather than conquest which stamps an imperial nation. And if our Empire melts away I think it will not be because we have lost the love of serving but because we have been denying that love to other people, so depriving them of a chance to practise virtues that could make them happy as much as they do us.

In Aden, during the first year of the war, while danger was creeping week by week towards us and the news with every bulletin grew worse, I realized how apt we are to do this. Arab ladies, sitting billowed in muslins, told me with a resigned air that they were prepared for death; and made me remember the Victorian ladies of Lucknow, forbidden to help in the hospital when the enemy's shot grew too threatening: "the women were denied even the simple pleasure of swaggering and their passive role was uniformly dreary." In Aden, the passive role extended to the whole local population, apart from a small nucleus of A.R.P. I realized the dreariness and tried to obtain permission for the young men to collect themselves into some sort of corps, to defend their streets and houses during raids. Even this modest aspiration was nearly as difficult as the female vote in its day. I was told that the young men of Aden were not needed; all they had to do was to wait quietly and be defended by people more competent than themselves. The point that service is good for the human soul seemed to meet a blank wall in the minds of devoted officials who in their own selves were working day and night for others. Eventually I did obtain the permission and the moral effect was good, and even the ladies turned their minds from impending death to the embroidering of armlets.

The history of the Indian Mutiny is illuminating in this matter, and one is inclined to forget that more than half the Lucknow garrison were Indian soldiers who remained devoted to the British cause.

"Lieutenant Aitken had meanwhile taken out a dozen of his sepoys from the Baillie Guard with picks and shovels to clear away the earthwork. Seeing dark faces in the dusk, the advancing Highlanders took them for mutineers and received them at the point of the bayonet. The sepoys made no resistance; three of them were wounded, and one of them said in the vernacular as he fell: 'Never mind, it was fated. Victory to the Baillie Guard!' The others lay on the ground crying: 'Aikeen Sahib! Aikeen Sahib!' until their commandant rushed up and shouted: 'For God's sake, don't harm these poor fellows, they've saved all our lives.'"*

I know India only from a six months' stay during the troubled year of 1945; but even in this short time I was puzzled by the difference in feeling between the civilian population and the army. Few would deny that outside the army our presence was objected to by most of the younger educated men and women; inside the army, few would affirm that we were disliked at all: and it seemed strange to me that we should be unwanted in a country that offered us the service of two million volunteers. The difference, I suggest, is to be found in this fact of service. Perhaps if the Viceroys could have been deified one after the other there would have been no trouble in a land that is happy bowing to its gods? As it is, the places of the gods were taken by army officers in the measure of their capacities, and the result was the same sort of surprising devotion that one receives from an Arab, or an old-fashioned retainer, or an Italian maid. Why should this virtue, which gives so much and asks for so little, be despised, so that the very word service is a stigma? The

* MICHAEL JOYCE. *Ordeal at Lucknow*, p. 235.

qualities of dominion have ousted it, and people like the Italians or Indians who are dedicated by nature, who have the warmth and the lovable kindness of *giving* in their bones, are made ashamed. Their virtue is a reproach and they turn away from it and become either abased or resentful; or try to acquire the admired autocratic qualities which make them unsuccessful and cruel.

Yet to service, which is the Cinderella among human qualities, the last gift of empire belongs; she conquers and is not feared. And perhaps we are all waiting for the moment when Autocracy and Bureaucracy, those domineering sisters, are put in their proper place by the kitchen fire, and the princes of this world find the little lost glass slipper of their neglected love.

3

HAPPINESS

           . . . all the vast
Unwearied ear of the whole universe
Listen'd in pain and pleasure at the birth
Of such new tuneful wonder.
                              KEATS. *Hyperion.*

The soul of man can by recognizing God draw Him into
its narrow boundaries, but also by love to Him itself
expand into the Infinite—and this is blessedness on earth.
    BURCKHARDT. *Civilization of the Italian Renaissance.*

For God mingles not with man; but through Love all the
intercourse and converse of God with man, whether awake
or asleep, is carried on.
                         PLATO. *Symposium.*

      The surety of its hidden root
      Has planted quiet in the night;
                    W. YEATS. *The Two Trees.*

things supreme in themselves, eternal, unnumber'd,
in the unexplored necessities of Life and Love.
        ROBERT BRIDGES. *Testament of Beauty*, I, 35.

A theme, recurring like music, half remembered, half
foreseen.
                    VIRGINIA WOOLF.

      . . . the rose remembers
      The dust from which it came.
                    EDNA ST. VINCENT MILLAY.

3 · HAPPINESS

MY father lived in a small wooden house in western Canada, where he carved himself out a fruit orchard from the hillside and the forest. He had chosen it with one of the most beautiful views in the world, an open valley and a river winding, with mountains beyond, and the Kootenay lake just visible in the north; and built himself a wide window, to look out on three sides. This window, and six Chippendale chairs which he had rescued in a farmer's sale, and a few of his sketches on the walls, were all the luxury of the place. I spent two winters with him, and once brought him a pot of primulas while the snow still lay heavy all around, but he soon took an occasion to say casually that he was not fond of forced plants: they took away something for him of the first rapture of the spring. His loves were very deep and gentle; they seemed not to be centred in islands of possession, like most human loves, but to be diffused among people and animals and plants, and even the shapes of things he saw; for he was a most sensitive artist. He lived among flowers and was first in his valley to send for bulbs from Holland and to fill his orchard with daffodils under the flowering trees. He was a good rider and a great walker and fond of the woodsmen and the hunters, and those who spend half the year away from their fellow men visiting traps in the mountain forests.

Four years before his death, when he was seventy-two, a stroke took away from him the open-air life he loved; and though by the strength of his will he managed, step by step with the passing months, to walk a mile or so with a stick to lean on, most of his time came to be spent in the window that looked out on his view. Here, he told me, the changing clouds and the light of the river would fill his mind with pleasantness for hours at a time and lead his thoughts into endless variation: and I believe this to be true, and that he was happy, for not only did he never complain, but his whole atmosphere was one of serenity and peaceful interest in all things as they came. And later, when I have thought of happiness and what it may be, I have always seen his gentle old head in the window, with the hillside full of tame pheasants and pigeons, and the valley and the mountains beyond, and have felt that the secret must have something in it of those older worlds which were as real to him as ours.

There is, of course, an animal contentment—the simple joy of running or sleeping or lying in the sun—whose deep and satisfying streams creep into our veins from ages far remoter than man. This is perhaps the oldest happiness. Love is almost as old, and older in this world than we are; there seems to me no reason to call the finer feelings instinct, and to think of them as different in kind from ours, when they belong to creatures other than ourselves. A few years before the war, the municipality of Venice awarded a medal and a daily saucer of milk to a cat, who lived in amity with a neighbour on the edge of the same canal. They had their litters of kittens at the same time, and no doubt shared adventures and gossip until the neighbour slipped one day and was drowned. Her friend dived and tried unsuccessfully to save her; she then adopted the orphan family and suckled it with her own; and the municipality of Venice recognized and rewarded her.

I once spent two months taming a small lizard rescued from Beduin Arabs of the south, till he ate from my hand and knew me. If he was frightened he would swell himself out to the shape of a miniature balloon and shrink again at the touch and safety of my hand. He had small bright triangular black eyes, and would hold his head on one side and look out of them with a Pan-like wisdom, gay and remote from ours, and —for me alone when I stroked him—these eyes turned suddenly round in their sockets; this is a strange but, according to books, natural way for lizards to express affection. The small reptile body had to die unless the sun's rays warmed a blood that runs differently from ours; yet human qualities of curiosity and courage were strangely vivid within it. He crouched, as still and small and flat as he could make himself, under the shadow of a bird overhead, or of an aeroplane which he obviously held to belong to the same species; but he was ready to pick up his meal where he left it as soon as the shadow had passed, and to run round the garden nibbling at plants he had never known before. As I watched him I found it pleasant to see these human things—courage, fear, affection, anger—tracing back to a pedigree so immensely more ancient than ours.

Who can say in what remoteness of time, in what difference of earthly shape, love first came to us as a stranger in the jungle? We, in our human family, know him through dependence in childhood, through possession in youth, through sorrow and loss in their season. In childhood we are happy to receive; it is the first opening of love. In youth we take and give, dedicate and possess—rapture and anguish are mingled, until parenthood brings a dedication that, to be happy, must ask for no return. All these are new horizons of content, which the lust of holding, the enemy of love, slowly contaminates. Loss, sorrow and separation come, sickness and death; possession, that tormented us, is nothing in our hands; it vanishes. Love's elusive enchantment, his ubiquitous presence, again become apparent; and in age we may reach a haven that asking for nothing knows how to enjoy. Perhaps the whole of life is a learning how to accept—to become as children and wiser, with hands outstretched and open, grasping nothing?

However this may be, we see that the happiness of every age is in this creature love, incomplete or growing according to its place. In the desert of the world he is the angel who guards our sleep in Time; whose ladder is planted on the early forms of things and stretches through us far beyond our vision, with rich and dangerous rungs. Almost alone of all earthly gifts, the gift of loving is shared with God.

Embracing the familiar, it looks out to the unknown and gazes like a child in its new world, with one hand ever for safety on the breast of earth its mother; and every revelation comes through some material door. A tendril of curl or curve of eyelash can unfold the universe: for the palpable

23

world is our window, and there is no end to the perspective of ordinary things; the scenes of our life constantly open upon regions to which themselves scarcely belong. Sometimes, in some stillness, the secret is all about us, never held but almost to be perceived. In such moments the individual ceases to be conscious of himself; he has dissolved the familiar, he is part of what he looks at, a part of Happiness: for an instant he has stepped into that ocean of which we are the scattered pools and these moments are never forgotten. They make our lives like journeys through the plain whose vaporous summer hides the mountain ranges; until one day, through some bite of autumn in the air the mist dissolves, and reality appears unexpected; the hills shine on the horizon, luminous and lightly shadowed like crumpled almond blossom transparent to the sun: the hidden summits are discovered, and ever afterwards we know that they are there.

I remember one such time on Mount Carmel, when in the sunset the sea was dove-grey, with a rosy light like the neck of a dove. From my stony height it looked burnished with innumerable ridges, but flat and wide so that Beato Angelico could have made angels walk there with hems lightly lifted, into the dying furnace of the sun. The sky was green jade, very pale; and there were clouds grey and white, the colour of ashes, and a slim moon, translucent as the wax of candles burning, and spanned as a thin eyebrow, or tartar bow. All these things were subdued, except the evening star; and that shone, not gold, but like an alloy of brass and silver and with its pale light stood in the van of the shadows of dusk.

The door is opened by beauty or pain, delight or sorrow, into a universe whose processes are not complete—a divine workshop where one can live in the active partnership of God.

Creativeness, too, we share with the divine in our degree: and because of this partnership which exists only in loving or creating, I believe that these two energies alone can give us happiness.

The power to create does not appear to have grown like love, slowly out of the building of earth; it is our Promethean gift. The delight of it is felt in its simple stages, by the child with his toy boat on the stream, by the mechanic over his screw, or the painter at his easel.   The wraith of this happiness still hovers on flint edges chipped evenly round the honey-coloured flakes men worked into axe or spear-head shapes in caves.   I have seen a woman in an Indian village painting round-bellied jars baked in a fire of dung, crouching with her skirts circular on the bare hard threshing floor, where the chaff dances in the dry wind and sun.   With one hand she held the jar, spanning its neck and pivoting it slowly on itself, while with the other, with grasses dipped in a mess of earth or ashes brown and white, she traced easy patterns that mankind has treasured throughout its prehistoric migrations.

I think the chain of continued creation makes the charm of old inhabited places and the melancholy of those fallen to ruin, which seem to testify to the waste of this best divinity in man.   It is certainly the charm of Italy, where the whole landscape has been altered and indeed almost fashioned by the chisel or the plough.   There is a grey keep crowning the little hill on which our town is settled; it looks like a windowless ark riding the last wave-crest of the small volcanic range which holds us; and its foundations are said to have been built, long before the Romans, by the Euganeans who left their name to another small volcanic range across the plain. Then the Romans must have made some *castrum* here, when they established us as a centre of government, and built baths beneath what is now the parish church, and a theatre in what is now my garden.   In the middle ages the keep grew to its present shape, with thin battlements against the sky, and a wedge of walls down the steep grass slopes to embrace the town; into which the Renaissance built painted houses with Venetian Gothic windows and columns cut in stone. All this we have adapted to our use and live happily on the tangle, looking out, to the plain or to the other hill slopes far and near, at other small towns and hamlets freshly blossoming out of their ancient past.   We look and realize that no other animal, except in a small way a beaver or an ant, has actually changed the appearance of the world as man is constantly doing.

Why should there be a quarrel between his past and future, between the tradition of his forgotten creativeness and his invention as it comes?   The substance of both is the same:

it is as if one footstep quarrelled with another on a slope where each climbs his own measure of the way.

But while there is pleasure in looking back over accomplishment, the word *happiness* must surely be reserved for that which actually allows us to share in the transformation. No mere knowledge, not even the acquisition of new knowledge, can give this firm delight. In it the amateur is joyful, the craftsman content, and the artist free of the weight of age. It is the secret of the pleasure women sometimes find in embroidery and men in gardens. Something is made, some combination of thoughts, materials, colours, which was not there before: imperfect as love, it shares with love the only divinity we have; it is our partnership in Creation.

4

EDUCATION

O fret not after knowledge—I have none,
And yet my song comes native with the warmth.
O fret not after knowledge—I have none,
And yet the Evening listens.

KEATS. *What the Thrush Said.*

In everything but disposition, they were admirably taught.

JANE AUSTEN. *Mansfield Park.*

"Ah, Mr. Fox," a friend said to him, "how delightful it
must be to loll along in the sun at your ease with a book
in your hand." "Why the book? why the book?" was
the reply.

ARTHUR BRYANT. *Years of Victory.*

Yet in spite of the decadence of the only two Universities
that then existed in England, in spite of the decay of the
endowed schools specially charged with secondary
education, the intellectual life of the country was never
more brilliant, and the proportion of men of genius per
head of population in the irregularly educated England
of George III was immensely greater than in our own day.

GEORGE TREVELYAN. *English Social History.*

The truth, my friends, is not eloquent, except unspoken;
its vast shadow lends eloquence to our sparks of thought
as they die into it.

GEORGE SANTAYANA. *Dialogues in Limbo.*

... there is simple ignorance, which is the source of lighter
offences, and double ignorance, which is accompanied by
a conceit of wisdom.

PLATO. *Laws,* IX.

4 . EDUCATION

OF the general inadequacy of intellect in the conduct of life Britain is the most majestic exponent. She is instinctively disliked by such people as French, Persians, Hindus, who are clever by nature, and think that *intellect can rule*. The Italians strayed down this path and disliked us too. But they, and the Greeks, and the Arabs, have a natural perception of other and greater powers and this, I think, is an affinity that binds us. With the others, with the intellectual, it is not our stupidity, but the fact that we prove it possible to live by non-intellectual standards, which makes us disliked.

If this is true, we may go on to say that intellect need not be the main object of education, and we join issue with half the modern world.

I have not been much educated myself, so that I am a puny fighter in the ring, but for better or worse I would like to have learnt four things when the passing bell puts an end to schooling, and of these one only can be called intellectual. I would like to command happiness; to recognize beauty; to value death; to increase, to my capacity, enjoyment. Around the cardinal points, and inevitably attained by their attainment, I should place the conquest of fear, whose elimination must be the final aim of teachers. The rest of education deals with technical means for living, and is of secondary importance whatever economists may say. It is chiefly because they have reversed our order and made the technical intellect supreme that we are suffering in the world to-day.

Three of my four aims are looked upon as extras in most schools. Happiness is known from her footprints to be divine;

she is free as air to the lovers and the craftsmen who share her secret; and the creature who *makes* or *loves* will know her, however poor the instrument on which he can perform. Love possibly is not a school product; but since the *maker* is the other child of happiness and few can use their minds alone for their creative labour, surely a great part of education should be the shaping of things with one's hands?

Beauty, too, like happiness, is no intellectual handmaid.

> Bow down, archangels, in your dim abode:
> Before you were, or any hearts to beat,
> Weary and kind one lingered by His seat;
> He made the world to be a grassy road
> Before her wandering feet.*

She is mistress in her own right. The connoisseur, expensively educated, looks on some early shape cradled by the uncultivated ancestors of man before metals were invented; and wonders what the secret is that gave so common and so sure a touch.

And who dares to be intellectual in the presence of death?

These all are children of eternity; but the last of my four aims comes, it seems to me, within the scope of a school curriculum, and is to be sought by intellectual means: for the object of learning ought to be the increase of enjoyment.

One of the reasons why there are so many discontented elderly people in England is that thinking, as a pleasure, has been unnoticed through their years. It has never received even the name of enjoyment, except sometimes among undergraduates, where it is looked upon as the cap or froth of youth soon to be shed; or among dons or the learned in general, where it is their job. That Alice-in-Wonderland key, which teaches us in infancy to sit and walk and hold and gradually to hear the rhythm of language and notice the variations of familiar things—we do not recognize it as the same intellectual instrument which in after life, if we but turn it, will continue to open door after door of unexpected gardens.

"On se lasse de tout, excepté de comprendre," says Anatole France. Alas! It is far more usual to get tired of under-

* W. YEATS. *The Rose of the World.*

30

OXFAM

VAT: 348 4542 38
**Donate your
preloved homeware
and help us
beat poverty**
www.oxfam.org.uk/shopvolunteer

ROBERT   SALES   F6406/POS1
WEDNESDAY 11 JULY 2018   13:42 053686

    NON FICTION   £1.99
    NON FICTION   £1.49

              2 Items

TOTAL   **£3.48**
CASH   £3.48

Oxfam Shop: F6406
45, High Street,
Unit 11, Elgin, IV30 1EE
01343 549908
oxfam.org.uk/shop

standing very soon. And why? Because the key is made to turn into dim passages, to be the access as it were to a basement of kitchen and plumbing, a menial key in fact.

This is unavoidable, says the economist: people have no time to waste if the world's work is to be done, and their living incidentally provided. And we may admit his plea and allow a certain amount of necessary dullness. But very few things are dull in their universal setting: the loss of their abiding perspective makes the monotony. In the profession of nursing, drudgery is enriched with a curtain of life and death so dramatic that interest envelops it and almost all nurses love their work: and we forget that nearly all business has these ramifications of life and death in a quiet way. Even the economist may agree that the strength of education is to provide perspectives that gild wayside puddles and common hours. It is not a matter of more time, but of changing the emphasis. The three-quarters of training are not in books at all; and the intellectual or bookish side, which keeps the world eating and working and furnishes learning and knowledge, should appear, even from childhood, as a detail in a landscape which stretches to infinite horizons, inhabited by older presences more intuitive and more august than printed words.

If this were so, we should be no worse than we are at our labours, and our years of intellectual education would never end. An old friend of mine near eighty learned Italian so that he might read Petrarch before he died. We would save up our spare hours as a woman saves odd moneys to variegate her wardrobe with a gown: so should we add sciences, or languages, or anything that gives a new joy; until such a treasure should be garnered in our active years as might suffice old age to combine and remember.

There was a string of beads I once coveted in a dingy little shop in Hamadan. They lay among never-dusted oddments in the window, and I had no idea that they were emeralds: they looked like irregular pebbles worn smooth and strung on a green silk cord; and what made me love them was their colour, transparent and undulating as water.

I was very poor, and it had been a long labour to save enough money to come to Hamadan. I sat there learning

Persian in the cold and early spring. A Frenchman, long exiled from his home, kept the hotel; it was rather down-at-heel but not unpleasantly dishevelled; and he tried to make love, I imagine, to all the female European travellers who passed by. There were not many; Hamadan had not then been tidied by Riza Shah; its main street tumbled down to the bazaar beside a torrent with one-arched, pointed bridges by Avicenna's tomb. On the cobbles, glutinous under mud, endless strings of donkeys with their noses slit for breathing (the people said) came from the slopes of Elvand or the plain. I worked at my Persian with an old Mirza for two hours every morning, and then put on gum boots and lost myself with delight in the dim entrancing tunnels of the bazaars, now long since cleared away. Every day I looked at the emerald window and at last went in to enquire, and discovered the price to be just about two guineas. Another month or more passed until, with the smallest economies, I carried my necklace home. It had been brought from the Urals by a Russian refugee and its green stones, smoothed by many hands, still delight me. Such stones of knowledge, it seems to me, we gather by intellectual labour and can hold in our hands, like the rosaries of the East, whose amber beads old men slip through their fingers, sitting at leisure, their harvests gathered, in the shade.

This is enjoyment, more laborious, less profound, less universal, less simple than happiness.

I have watched the contrast of the two in Chicago, where the sight of a happy man is unusual, so that one notices it. He was a Greek, master of a small eating place to which comfortable business men and women came from their offices nearby. They ate as a matter of course, thinking of other things, with strident voices. The Greek, his face lined and eager, bent over every table to ask how they had liked the rather indifferent food: he did not do this as a matter of routine; he had cooked it all, and he loved them for tasting it; and his face showed a sort of radiance over the result. The contrast of what he put into this daily creation and the response among the young clerks was so remarkable that, when the old man reached me, I asked him about himself and heard how he had come in his youth from Napulia,

32

in sight of Argos and the sea; and was contented in Chicago, as indeed he would be anywhere, since the root of the matter was in his heart.

With this happiness in mind we face the economists who rule our world; and tell them that the aim of intellectual education is to increase enjoyment, and that it is therefore not something to finish with adolescence, but to continue, with available leisure, so that a gentle movement of fresh thoughts be ever with us, diminishing as the volume of our treasure increases, but still there like the current through a pond that prevents stagnation, right into the stiffness of age; and that this intellectual enjoyment is in itself a part only, and a small part, of education, whose other branches feed in a vaster air, of happiness, beauty or death.

These regions are beyond the intellectual grasp and the school's neglect; they accept no curriculum. But their presence is so radical, and the human need of them so profound, that much—it seems—could be accomplished not by an alteration of things taught, but by a change in the angle of the teaching. The exactness of knowledge is the anteroom: beyond the classroom threshold, the presence chambers shine with dim gold, and all can walk or wander there. This should be the fact which education teaches and which, if we remember, is all that is essential to know.

There, in the majesty of something greater than ourselves, equality is born. For book knowledge can be more or less according to advantage or opportunity; but these inarticulate and subconscious realms have other rivers from which all men, in their moments, can drink their fill. In time of need leaders and orators remember them and, perhaps without knowing, grope towards them and find them, like Nile-flooded monuments, firmly bedded and surely founded beneath the ooze of fashions; their fair stone steps and edges will endure uncorroded, long after our annual academic floods have spent themselves and passed.

5

BEAUTY

Verily her most inferior pearl brightens the East and West.
(Abu Sa'id's tradition of the Houri of Paradise.)

... the Gods, who, as we say, have been appointed to be
our companions in the dance, have given the pleasurable
sense of harmony and rhythm;

PLATO. *Laws*, II.

And as an ev'ning dragon came.

MILTON. *Samson Agonistes*.

Mòstrasi sî piacente a chi la mira
Che dà per gli occhi una dolcezza al core,
Che'ntender no la può chi no la prova.
E par che de la sua labbia sî mova
Un spiritel soave pien d'amore,
Che va dicendo a l'anima: "Sospira!"

DANTE. *Vita Nuova*.

Il est difficile d'être insensible quand on pense vivement,
et c'est pour la plupart des hommes un example dé-
courageant que la sérénité d'un cochon.

ANATOLE FRANCE. *Vie Litt.*, II.

I find under the boughs of love and hate,
In all poor foolish things that live a day,
Eternal beauty wandering on her way.

W. YEATS. *To the Rose upon the Rood of Time*.

There is no excellent beauty that hath not some strangeness in the proportion.

BACON.

... like the morning star
Amid the weary stars of night.

WILLIAM MORRIS. *Earthly Paradise*.

5 . BEAUTY

Long ago, when the world seemed safe—in the spring of 1914—my mother and I spent three weeks walking down the Adriatic coast from Venice to Ravenna.

We went by water to Chioggia, where in the evening the houses look like mother-of-pearl reflected in the lagoon. From there we crossed the mouths of Brenta by pale green spits of land and walked among crops and slow canals, whose water plants grow rank in mud, and by small prosperous towns that once were harbours, now long forgotten of the sea. Such is Adria, asleep in the sun, unaware of the salt wastes and wearing currents with which her name is tied. And from Adria we came to Rovigo, which has not even the wraith of a name that men remember but lives obscure and prosperous, busy with weekly markets and the fluctuations of corn.

Here we spent two days in a rambling hotel that must once have been a town house of importance, for the bedrooms had tessellated floors, and doors with frames carved and gilded, branching up to vague pictures in the dimness of vaulted ceilings. From here, after a sleep in the afternoon, one might walk to the piazza, to sit at whichever of two cafés happened to be in shadow: the three-legged tin tables, painted brown in imitation—one must imagine—of linoleum, overflowed on to the pavement, where the warmth of the morning's sun still lay lethargic, like a domestic atmosphere long past its best.

The bourgeoisie of Rovigo liked to sit there passive in the shade and, when we first arrived, we found them gathered in both cafés to watch some wandering acrobats at their show.

The piazza was rectangular and narrow and the artists

had slung a rope from house roofs on either side; so that we sat and sipped our grenadine and looked up at them as they walked in coloured satins into the summer sky. The rope trembled; they tested it with their padded shoes and then advanced with tense defiant ease, a parasol—and eventually a bicycle—in one hand. Their ancestors must have done this before the eyes of Veronese or Tintoretto, to produce those hurtling figures from painted heavens: one felt that at any moment they might become Tintoret in motion, with head instead of feet foreshortened. They came and went for our amusement, while a brass tray circulated among our tables in the square to collect what we wished to give. I thought gruesomely how ugly they would be suspended there if they were dead. But they were life triumphant, safely walking the thread between earth and heaven, and so beautiful that the sight is with me to-day. I have thought about it often, and pictured those figures in their cheap bright satins as types of the essence of beauty, so slightly balanced yet dependent.

Beauty walks along the edge of opposites, between pattern and freedom. If pattern is too strong, the play of fancy ceases, and beauty with it; we foster rigid fashion and imitative arts. If freedom swings too wide we are lost in air.

Fashion shows how delicate the balance must be; the Parisienne observes it, holding the line of the year or the moment—with subtle touches making it her own. See her trying on a hat, consulting with the maker over every quarter-inch of brim or subtle elevation, passionately conscious of that breath, that nothing, that gossamer balance which keeps the meaning of an hour's fancy steady in the perpetual fluidity of temporal affairs.

This balance makes the loveliness of motion—of running or diving, or the flight of birds. Control is essential behind it, for with a wounded bird or a drunken man staggering, beauty ceases. It is the artist's secret. The sonnet triumphantly weaves fancy into the rigid form; and the freest *vers libres* must have that discipline if they are to live. In architecture, where landscape is a part of the picture, any break in the balance is offensively clear.

By this unseen test of pattern, the use of ornament is regu-

lated in art. When decoration predominates unduly it is a
sign of civilization declining: people are no longer aware of the
thing they wish to say. In our age we go to the opposite extreme
and are afraid of ornament, thinking to keep pure by simplicity
which, in this case, is but a bankrupt name: for the great
ones need not trouble to be simple; the substance of what
they are creating keeps them in their course. They can
play with waves as they come, or make a wide tack of fancy
to their harbour—the feel of their hand on the rudder is
secure.

Perhaps this union of pattern and freedom helps to explain
the strange quality of beauty—its independence of the ingredients which make it; for it is an addition, a visitor, a
surprise; it sips where the bee sips and is off. Kindness is
made up of kind parts, and anger of the elements of anger;
the moral qualities hold together in a reasonable way. But
beauty lights on incongruous things which are separately
nothing, and throws a net of gossamer and is there: the hay-
stack, or old cropping horse in a dull field, or some mere
shabby line of ditch or wall are caught by a random slanting
beam into a glory which is non-existent in any of its parts.
In the same way, when every piece is perfect, their union may
disintegrate the magic: the elusive Ariel has fled.

Though beauty does not mean happiness, it is often found
where happiness abides. And this, too, is strange about it
and separates it from other qualities—that it is not recognized
in a general fashion, but appears in different ways to all men,
and differently even to the same man at different times. It
comforts when all else fails in the house of sorrow, and breaks
the silence there with its own more gentle silence, and soothes
returning life into the limbs of pain. Plato thinks of it as a
memory, seen fragmentarily and speaking to our hearts with
sudden poignance of what they once have known. I am no
philosopher and would not venture so deeply: yet I too, and
nearly all human beings, I imagine, have felt that lightness
as it were of recognition, which may be memory, or may also
be, in the cosmic jigsaw, the sort of pleasure one has in finding
two pieces that suddenly fit: they make no exact sense, but
their joining brings us nearer to the understanding of the
whole.

The two threads of pattern and freedom are a part not only of beauty but of life; the Fates spin them into a double skein and twist them close. On this side of the human threshold they tie all arts and creatures in their subtle bond, and if we cannot see the same bond clearly beyond humanity, we can yet, I believe, find traces of it here and there, in a universe whose patterns and whose freedoms must be so far beyond the scope of our regard.

Such a trace, I often feel, is the horizon, which hems the diversity of landscape in its geometric band; the beauty of prospects would be sadly shorn without that meeting of variety and law. Such too is the harmony of houses with the land in which they are set, so that it is ever rash to build with foreign stone: and the hidden link of birds migrating, or of flowers that cannot look happy with leaves other than their own, as if the same sap were needed to run through the green background and its climax of colour: all these appear to be links in a hidden chain of harmonies at which we guess in default of knowledge, and add beauty to nature by the remembrance of Law; so that the world we look on is more complicated and richer than that of the other creatures, so far as we can tell. One of the most haunting sentences in the English language is that in which Coleridge, in *The Ancient Mariner*, describes the stars:

> In his loneliness and fixedness he yearneth towards the journeying Moon, and the stars that still sojourn, yet still move onward; and everywhere the blue sky belongs to them, and is their appointed rest, and their native country and their own natural homes, which they enter unannounced, as lords that are certainly expected and yet there is a silent joy at their arrival.

How differently would this have been written, if it were not for the feeling behind it of the ordered procession, the eternal rhythm, the immense order. And what traveller, sleeping in mountains or desert, has not felt this awe of beauty under the tented sapphire night?

If loveliness is so engaged, as I believe, in the skein of our universe, it is sad that it should be little cared for in our schools.

The whole of the industrial world proclaims its unimportance, and millions and millions of people spend their lives looking almost exclusively at ugly things. This surely will pass. What is more insidiously dangerous at the moment is a timid heresy which believes that the ignorant can be trained to beauty by the second-rate. The fallacy of our age maintains it better to do things badly than not at all. As a matter of fact there is very little harm in doing nothing: to do things badly is an active getting in the way of the few necessary people who might do good. To adapt beauty to "the man in the street" is to use the bed of Procrustes with a vengeance and to mutilate divinity: it is better to remember that the man in the street himself was made in the likeness of God. To him beauty is simple and easy, a natural hunger which all can assimilate in elementary or complicated form, provided they are not cluttered up with mediocrity already. Mediocrity will never lead to beauty: the two roads are not even parallel; they are divergent.

Who cannot think of many instances of this patient hunger among poor people, so meagrely satisfied in our towns? I remember a man, on a spring day, in Regent's Park: he leant with his elbows on a railing, and might have been on the dole, so ragged and shapeless were his clothes. He was gazing into a bush of escalonia in flower, and was unaware of my passing close by him: he was unaware of everything in the world except the dewy tents of blossom, and looked like Dante when Beatrice came to him at the gates of Paradise.

One of the comforts of life in our hill town is that such heritage of loveliness as we have is shared by all. Beauty gives the saving grace and passion to the Italian character. When the Allies last year commandeered most of the steamers that ply the Grand Canal in Venice, and thereby caused no end of inconvenience to the population, the grievance was more than doubled by the painting of the steamers red and green, a constant hideous blot against a background lovely in origin and enhanced by time. And a friend of mine told me that his gondolier, a communist, once delayed him and rested on his oar below Rialto while he shouted abuse to the unseen inhabitants of an upper window who were defacing, with washing, the symmetry of the Grand Canal.

The time will come when we shall understand that beauty is no farmyard animal to be fattened at a manger, subservient to a price. One cannot make people live in ugly sites, and turn on culture in a museum, and think it will work. In the *Iliad*, the anger of Achilles is *terrible as the morning star*: this is beauty indeed: the young lover sees it with fear and rapture, dawning in the eyes of his beloved, "*terrible as an army with banners.*" Such is all beauty—a pleasure and a pain, the flash of an opening window into depths upon depths of light, a revelation of awe. But awe is not taught in our schools: economic men have forgotten that these are gods that we harness, though science cannot tell whence they come or what they are, and Socrates by the Ilyssus knew as much as we.

During the summer of 1944 I had a month's leave, and I was among the few people who stayed in London for pleasure. V.1 were striking at us like the arrows of Apollo. By day one saw the short sinister bodies as they jerked through cloud; by night one tracked them low over the London roofs by their trail of flame. I had a window opening widely to the south, and sometimes watched three at a time; they were heralded by the siren's moan, and clanked like armour; and if, as I lay in bed, the noise drew very near, I would cover my face with the pillow and wait, and think how the visible gods, alien and unforgiving, once walked booted with terror over the cowering and darkened homes of Troy. And then I would think that perhaps we too might do well to attribute the ills from which we suffer to some neglect or carelessness towards our gods.

6

DEATH

For the young heart like the spring wind grows cold
And the dust, the shining racer, is overtaking
The laughing young people who are running like fillies
The golden ladies and the ragpickers
And the foolish companions of spring, the wild wood
lilies.

EDITH SITWELL, *Green Song.*

And he, like all great souls, lived and loved, conscious
every day of the price, which is death.

ALICE MEYNELL. *Mrs. Dingley.*

This was the last word of the tale, when sweet sleep came
speedily upon him . . . unknitting the cares of his soul.

Odyssey.

. . . and desire shall fail: because man goeth to his long
home.

Ecclesiastes xii. 5.

Atque erit illa mihi mortis honesta dies.

PROPERTIUS.

Il n'y a pas de régles pour mourir d'une blessure, même
dans l'état militaire, ou l'éxactitude est poussée à ses
dernières limites.

ANATOLE FRANCE. *La Reine Pédoque.*

The great tragedy of life is not that men perish but that
they cease to live.

ANON.

And none of those who dwell there desire to depart thence,
—no, not even the Sirens; but even they, the seducers, are
there themselves beguiled, and they who lulled all men,
themselves laid to rest—they, and all others—such sweet
songs doth death know how to sing to them.

PLATO. *Cratylus: John Ruskin's translation.*

6 . DEATH

PICTURES of one's childhood are as fragmentary as the relics of the sailor's way which wanders through the south of England; a stretch emerges here and there, though most of it has vanished or been transformed. Amid these half-obliterated memories I can see, quite sharply, my first meeting with the image of death.

I must have been about four years old and a nurse in our grandmother's house was putting me to bed. It was a Victorian house where fireplaces had tall brass fenders highly polished, and the black metal bed-rails ended in knobs of brass; many pillows, beginning with bolsters, were piled up towards a chintz canopy from which curtains descended, securely lined against draughts, tied with tasselled ropes of red and green. Standing there on the eiderdown, being buttoned into a long nightgown that lay about my feet, I asked if my mother would live for ever.

"No," said nurse, "not for ever; but for a long time."

"How long?" said I. "A thousand years?"

"No," said nurse. "Not a thousand years."

The finality of Time was borne in upon me. Hours afterwards my parents, coming up to bed, found me half asleep but still sobbing at the top of the stairs, where I had crept a little nearer to those dear ones who in a thousand years would be dead.

This feeling has never really changed. If the world is not to last for ever, it seems to make no difference whether its time is to be counted in millions or billions of years; what matters is that there is an end. There can be no safe happiness until the fact has been faced and assimilated; and an

45

absolute condition of all successful living, whether for an individual or a nation, is the acceptance of death.

What remnant of old darkness makes us fear? In all things else we recognize the values of black and white, the strength of contrast.

> Night, the shadow of light,
> And life, the shadow of death.*

Death, too, is an enhancer. Through him, life gains its colour, clinging precarious like some Alpine flower that digs its tenuous and tenacious roots in the rock face against the darkness of the drop below. The secret joy of peril comes from the veiled presence, without which most savour goes; and this is no morbid feeling, for the ecstasy belongs not to death in itself, but to *life*, suddenly enriched to know itself alive. So, after a summer dawn and climb till noon, among clefts and icy triangles or wind-scooped crannies, the mountaineer returning sets foot again on the short turf and flowers; and the breeze that cools him is the same breeze that sways the harebells; the blood that tramples in his ears and runs like chariots through his veins is the kind, swift, temporary stuff by which the smaller things of earth are fed; he is back in the community of his kind and descends, light-footed, among the pastures: but he remembers how in the high silences he has known himself on the edge of Silence and how its wing has brushed him. Once, looking down into a valley of the Lebanon, I have heard below me as it were a swish of silk and seen, within a pebble's drop, an eagle's wings outspread; and so we watch death's flight, in our sunlight.

The presence enters far more than one would imagine into commonplace things. Last year, in the cold that comes with the lengthening days, Turin kept her first carnival after the war among her bombed streets and dingy snows; and a wide square was filled in the pale winter daylight with merry-go-rounds and bumping motor-bugs, toy-stands, and sweetmeat booths, and swings. The most popular show was in a wooden cylinder built like a tower, about thirty feet both in breadth and height. We paid to climb by a wooden stair and to look down to where a young blonde, dressed like a Johann

* SWINBURNE. *Atalanta in Calydon.*

Strauss hussar, stood waiting beside a motor bicycle in a pit below. One push with her neat black boot on the sanded floor, and she was off, climbing vertical at first and then gradually horizontal, in quickening spirals, round the smooth plank sides towards her audience. The wooden tower resounded, swaying to the thumps of the engine, and with every hissing upward curve the crowd against the parapet drew back. Another female hussar soon appeared on another motor bicycle. They raced each other; they vied in audacity; they sat with arms akimbo, or placed a booted foot upon the handlebars:

> With life before and after
> And death beneath and above,*

It was a picture of our own existence—the progress of every creature on this earth between two gulfs of time. And did we not pay our sixpences in order, obscurely, to feel this foundation of ourselves?

Why, then, should there be a desire to keep from children the knowledge of death? When once it is obtained, all else falls into perspective; it is the chord to which the music of our life is played. No depth, no harmony, no realizing even of happiness, is possible without it. It makes the grace and dignity of small and trivial things.

> My darling's sparrow is dead:
> The sparrow she delighted in
> And loved more than her eyes.
> For it was honey-sweet and knew her
> As a child knows its mother;
> Nor strayed from her lap,
> But hopping here and there,
> Piped only to its lady.
> And now walks the dark way
> Whence all are forbidden return.
> Ah, evil be upon you, dark evil
> Monsters, who devour all lovely things.
> You have taken from me the pretty sparrow.
> O evil deed! O luckless sparrow!
> Now by your doing my darling
> Has reddened and swollen her sweet eyes with tears.†

* SWINBURNE. *Atalanta in Calydon.*   † CATULLUS. *Lesbia's Sparrow.*

Great literature is saturated with a consciousness of death, which may come with personal directness as it did to Keats, when he woke with a spot of blood upon his pillow and recognized the sign:

> When I behold, upon the night's starr'd face,
> Huge cloudy symbols of a high romance,
> And think that I may never live to trace
> Their shadows, with the magic hand of chance;*

Or the power of imagination alone may be sufficient. How it comes matters little; but the existence of the vision of death gives life and beauty to this world. This is the happy reason that carries humanity singing across the dark ages; and those are fortunate who see it early so that they may enjoy a sense of proportion for the remainder of their days. An awareness of death is as essential in education as the study of happiness, or beauty, or intellectual enjoyment.

Whether or no it is accompanied by a belief in future life, appears to be less important. Unbelievers face their end as peacefully as Christians, and the fear of death is independent of rational guidance. It is a fear that in sickness comes closer, like a long wave shining in the sun; its immense ridge gathers unavoidable, a vanguard of the sea; and terrifies as it approaches, and towers with facets of light over its darkening curve. But many that have been under its shadow and watched it breaking and felt its fear have suddenly known it to be no more than a physical barrier, a mere reluctance in their departure from familiar things; and tranquillity has come in sight beyond the aimless foam. If one can hold to the remembrance of such a revelation, one may hope to be free for ever.

No nation can be great, or even respectable, until it achieves such freedom; and it seems to me that the fault of our literature, and of much of our thought between the two wars, was the fear and distortion of death; so that when our moment came there was a good deal of uncertainty in what should have been the intellectual leadership of England. There is an emphasis on carnage in the poets who came after 1914

* KEATS. Sonnet.

48

which is surely out of all proportion; for the horror of death and destruction is not in the thing itself but in the causes that bring it about. A book like *Cry Havoc* gives despicable reasons for disliking war; and the wise pacifist should be careful not to let even the hem of his argument flutter in the wind of fear. If peace cannot teach us that death is harmless, then war will ever be a benefit in some degree: and for this reason if for no other, such sports as riding, climbing, sailing, are better for children than games: for they help to show them, in a light of danger, their universe suspended, as it were a shield or an armorial bearing on some old gate of time—to whose quarterings and crest the ancient sculptors have given a place of honour, supported by two allegoric figures, that hold the weight of the shield between them, on brotherly arms outstretched. Such old and decorated gateways can be seen all over the Italian countryside, and I think of the two figures, baroque and ruinous but gay—as Life and Death, with our world and all its pomp held up between them.

7

MEMORY

Wide sea, that one continuous murmur breeds
Along the pebbled shore of memory!

KEATS. Endymion, II.

Mr. Walpole says, our memory sees more than our eyes in
this country.

THOMAS GRAY. Letters.

. . . and in the light of light
man's little works, strewn on the sands of time, sparkle
like cut jewels in the beatitude of God's countenance.

ROBERT BRIDGES. Testament of Beauty, II, 506

O moon, how many evening glances have visited you!
O branch, how many singing nightingales have you
borne!

From the Arabic.

The alphabet, trickling from its humble source as a kind
of phonetic mnemonic device, useful to such poor devils
as had no time to memorize a thousand pictographs, had
become the very Nile along whose fertile banks all
Western civilizations had clustered.

The Times Literary Supplement. 20.1.40.

We cannot say the past is past without surrendering the
future.

WINSTON CHURCHILL.

. . . the rose's scent is bitterness to him that loved the rose.

FRANCIS THOMPSON.

I cannot tell what crop may clothe the hills,
The merry hills Troy whitened long ago.

WILLIAM MORRIS. The Earthly Paradise.

7. MEMORY

SOME words come heavily jewelled out of their history. Feelings and thoughts have been encrusted on them in their passage through centuries and nations, and Oxus

> Rejoicing, through the hush'd Chorasmian waste
> Under the solitary moon;*

carries a siren magic; there is, as it were, a patina of old bronze produced by use and time. This jewelled quality of language gives richness to literature. It gives to words the same atmosphere that a house acquires by being loved and lived in—whose magnificence is not expressed but latent, and belongs neither to the builder nor to the present user of the dwelling; but has been gathered unconsciously by those who, in careless generations, have played and used and left the mark of their lives upon their symbols.

Pleasure, too, has the acquired quality, the polish of repeated use, so that there is difference like that of childhood and age between new and remembered delight. I have never been able to determine their respective claims. Whether for instance, on a holiday, it is better to revisit or to explore? The passing of time decides for us; and part of the content-ment of age with its own walks and gardens comes from an increase of riches, the accumulated capital, as it were, which the mind in its journey has collected; so that every note of the small instrument we play on becomes an orchestra in itself, and links and wreathes into a wealth of undertones the melodies and half-forgotten snatches of our past.

* M. ARNOLD. *Sohrab and Rustum.*

No nightingale did ever chaunt
Such welcome notes to weary bands
Of travellers in some shady haunt
Among Arabian sands:
Such thrilling voice was never heard
In spring-time from the cuckoo-bird,
Breaking the silence of the seas
Among the farthest Hebrides.*

In Kurdistan I have heard the sudden call of the cuckoo
from some dell encircled and sheltered by precipices and
hidden in walnut trees, among hills white in the sun like
bones. The poor notes, shrill and naked in themselves,
brought an English edge of woodland and lush paths, and the
afternoons that slope to twilight with the lengthening days;
and in the train of these, the songs of poets and echo of that
pleasure which their words first gave. Now to all this richness is added the Kurdish landscape with its gaunt ridges and
warlike remote life, that comes to me when the cuckoo sings
in June among the Asolo hills.

Such is pleasure, so linked and enriched with all that
goes before it until, like a piece of embroidery, the stuff on
which it is stitched is hidden beneath the silken threads—
threads of our own life's countless moments, and threads of
gold, spoken or sung or painted by those immortals who
weave themselves into our pattern regardless of time. The
pleasure which first we feel is a storehouse for all the repeti-
tions of itself. And it is well to take our feelings as fully and
as deeply and in as great a variety as we can in our youth,
since they are the capital on whose interest the rest of our
life will flourish: for the kind dispensation has permitted
nearly all agreeable things to gain an access of grace through
memory, while the disagreeable withhold their unpleasantness and, unaided, are easily and soon forgotten.

The charm of presents, for instance, lies in a magic only
accidentally connected with the object, whatever it may be.
I am particularly delighted with scented things that one can
use daily, and in their little shock of repeated delight think
kindly of the sender: without such personal addition, there

* W. WORDSWORTH. *The Solitary Reaper.*

is a poverty in the most ravishing perfume; and I daresay it is this feeling of delight enriched by memory and so easily repeated, which has made perfume acceptable as a gift to women from the days of the Queen of Sheba and before.

Among the peoples of the world memories held in common, that build themselves like coral islands from generation to generation, create a barrier of nationalism: for what is there in human beings to differentiate one from another in their essential qualities except their past? Like the words of their speech, the flags of nations go by heavy with encrusted meanings, the dust and stains of battlefields whose history is forgotten though the marks remain; they hang in the cathedrals of their people, whom they stir because of these old rents of war; and a new flag speaks as little as a new-coined word to the heart.

In smaller, more familiar things, memory weaves her strongest enchantments, holding us at her mercy with some trifle, some echo, a tone of voice, a scent of tar and seaweed on the quay; we have all been explorers in our time, even if it was only when we learned to walk upon unsteady feet on the new carpet of our world; and it is those forgotten explorations that come back, intruding all about us in the ordinary routine of our lives. This surely is the meaning of home—a place where every day is multiplied by days before it. The edifice can be created at any age, by an accumulation of happiness and time; but it is rare in later life to drink such draughts as we do in childhood of the world's wonder, whose first depth remains through all our days.

In Devonshire, where my parents lived for many years, old oak woods and fir plantations stretched up from the back of the house towards the moors. The oak trees were mossy with comfortable branches, and a yellow-green light filtered there in a friendly way, hanging as in cathedral aisles among the fretted leaves and airy domes; but the fir plantations were silent and private, little inhabited by birds and too closely grown for winds to toss or sun to visit; a fear, a sort of taboo brooded in their straight darkness carpeted with moss and starred with still and muddy pools; and beyond them, the heart lifted at a sudden clearing, where boulders of speckled granite were piled in a weatherbeaten wall against the moors.

Here the bracken washed up the hillside with fronds shiny as the sea, and young shoots unfolded in a Byzantine curl of waves, and the whole expanse bent when the south wind blew; and at one step from the path the serrated canopies met above one's head, opening in fanlike traceries like the vaulting at Christ Church, and leading in endless avenues of stems to the Unknown. No exploration I have ever shared in has been more rich than this in delight and wonder, which still linger when I see the bracken in a woodland clearing, though tame now and flat and shrunken in my sight.

Love, too, and even more so friendship, are built by memory in this small persistent way. After our first vision of them, the persons we care for become composite beings, altered by every meeting as it comes so that they really exist less in the present than in the past, and are embodiments not only of their own but also of *our* departed days: the ingredients of them, as far as we are concerned, are all the gathered occasions, mostly forgotten, in which our lives have joined.

This is what makes absence so dangerous a menace to love, for the creature we meet again is no longer the one whose image lay like the sleeping princess in our heart; she is awake, and alarmingly different; and who can blame anyone for being unable to live on memories that have ceased to tally with the facts? The wise lover follows the French poet:

> J'ai trouvé le secret
> De t'aimer
> Toujours pour la première fois.*

Constancy is a static virtue; the delight which we have seen moving like wind through our loves and pleasures is here recollected in a state of apotheosis and apt to be deified into stone. "All the privilege I claim for my own sex," says Anne Elliot, in that memorable conversation with Captain Harville, ". . . is that of loving longest, when existence or when hope is gone!"†

Even the most inconstant are faithful in their way, and

* ANDRÉ BRETON.
† JANE AUSTEN. *Persuasion*

through the varied pageant of their loves see and pursue again and again the first and fleeting splendour. To most of us some stranger, in the press of the world, with a mere glance, a gesture, an expression, will suddenly wring our heart out of the depths of its days; dead love, like a drowned face, then rises to the surface of our stream. There is no rule for constancy: if recollection is rich enough to satisfy, that is happiness sufficient: if the harvest is poor, if bare patches begin to appear in those private fields so often tilled—why then let us remember that Experience is like the marshal's baton, a potential fortune at the bottom of every knapsack in the world, a treasure of which hope is the key. So Dr. Johnson appeared to think, when on the subject of widowers and wives. The truth is that constancy of a sort is an unescapable virtue; for the things that the heart is seeking, if they are multiple at all, are very few; they are found and lost many times over with changing names: the young explorer looks for them and the old lover remembers; and the difference between them is not so great.

For when its wonder of infancy was over, Memory began to take all human things, and warmed them and made them pliable as wax, and modelled them anew; altering the meaning of words and of banners, and the buildings of love; giving a value to pleasure and a halo to sorrow and joy. In the garment of memory man is encased like a grain of wheat in the sheaf of the ear, and the two are indistinguishable in the russet of the harvest.

8

INDIVIDUALS

. . . le bien public est formé d'un grand nombre de maux particuliers.

ANATOLE FRANCE. *Opinions de Jérôme Coignard.*

Abu Hurairah said, "Verily the Apostle of God said, when an Arab was sitting near him, that a man of the people of Paradise will ask permission of his Lord to cultivate land and God will say: 'Have you not everything you could wish for? What will you cultivate?' The man will say: 'Yes, everything is present, but I am fond of cultivating.' Then he will be permitted to cultivate."

TRADITION.

It is our Institutions that have made us free, and can alone keep us so; by the bulwark which they offer to the insidious encroachment of a convenient, yet enervating, system of centralization, which, if left unchecked, will prove fatal to the national character.

DISRAELI. Moneypenny and Buckle: *Life of Disraeli.*

. . . the strongest motive power in the world—the force of genius untrammelled by the rule of mediocrity.

ARTHUR BRYANT. *Years of Endurance.*

With all their perseverance in study and in religion, the Irish kept their minds free: at any moment they could hear and take pleasure in the liveliness of the real world, and no theology nor moral law could prevent them from seeing the fun of it.

W. P. KER. *The Dark Ages.*

. . . and his poor friend Fipps, who went mad and ran about the country with an axe, hacking branches off the trees whenever there were not the same number on both sides.

G. K. CHESTERTON, *Napoleon of Notting Hill.*

as to the walls, Megillus, I agree with Sparta in thinking that they should be allowed to sleep in the earth,

PLATO. *Laws,* VI.

8 · INDIVIDUALS

IN Burckhardt's *Civilization of the Renaissance in Italy* it is said
that at one time there were no fashions in the dress of
Florence; individual taste was so well thought of that
everyone preferred to invent a personal style of his own.

Even now, in a debased and scattered form, this independence survives in small Italian towns and country places;
how long it will hold up its head against the mass-produced
invasion is very uncertain, but while it still exists it gives
its stamp of humanity to business dealings. It encour-
ages an expenditure of time and an area of unexpectedness,
like the white spaces of a map; this is pleasant or irritating
according to your temperament; but it does produce a
world where one object is different from another, whether
it be the dresses of the women, stitched and rearranged by
themselves out of last year's wardrobe, or whether it be the
lamps, the glass, the jewels set to your taste, or the furniture
sketched to your design, and finished well or badly according
to the local carpenter's genius in his shop.

In Asolo the shops are mostly set back in arcades on the
ground floor of what were once fine houses; from the entrances,
suddenly dark, one looks through to where workmen and
apprentice bend silhouetted against a sunlit space, whose
sheaves of light lie on the plain below. One brushes by
stacked wares dusty and familiar, to discuss the making of a
gown or the inches of a cornice, or the exact line that places a
new window pleasantly in the middle of a wall. The rich
have an architect or designer, but most of us do it ourselves;
in either case, it is a co-operation between him who makes and
him who orders, a small affair of give and take and consulta-

INDIVIDUALS

tion between man and man. Now the huge sweep of war, large economic or totalitarian vistas, have rushed into the foreground of this landscape made up of little and individual things: Italian ceramics, silks, embroideries, though still made by hand, are being churned out in a symmetry as swift, cheap, and impersonal as their nature allows. The maker will be truculent about it. "The new fashion," he will say. But if you stick to your point and maintain that the fashion, however new, is *ugly*, the old feeling of the centuries still tells—the man in his apron, with the pleasant face and the clever hands of the craftsman, looks sadly at the horrid little objects he produces. "We know them to be ugly," he says. "But They want them, and we have to live."

I often wonder what is wrong with mass production, whose cheapness and ease of making allows innumerable people to enjoy the otherwise unattainable. The mosaics of Ravenna show that one can yet be beautiful while standing in a row; it is something more profound than similarity which takes loveliness away. We do not enjoy the sight of electric lamps upon our altars: for though candles are but mutton fat and tallow, or perhaps wax that the bees have swallowed, yet in their burning *they are consumed*; their waste makes them precious and more dear to us than the nimble, immortal, invulnerable lightnings which we tame: and the parable of the box of ointments still holds.

True religion teaches wastefulness, and how easily and smugly we forget it.

> O, reason not the need: our basest beggars
> Are in the poorest thing superfluous:
> Allow not nature more than nature needs,
> Man's life is cheap as beast's.*

Nearly every manufactured thing that we handle is an extra to the necessities of life, whose natural bareness one has only to be a prisoner or a desert traveller to remember. We have spent all our history in complicating this essential simplicity: and sometimes I take in my hands some common object, a cup or kerchief or a reel of thread, and think of it in terms of

* SHAKESPEARE. *King Lear*, II. iv.

the lives that have elaborated it and brought it through to us, until its homely familiar outlines grow majestic in the mere pyramid of time. The things used day by day and left by chance prove the steps of the human journey, like a lantern flickering by night that lurches in darkness and disappears and re-emerges, and shows where the invisible pathway runs.

The whole charm of archaeology lies in the finding of these tangible links of objects in the human chain, and the using of them as clues to recapture a brotherhood lost in its years. I have a spoon with a twisted handle, and a button—a small convex circle rather like a military button to-day, but smooth and thinly beaten out of bronze. They were tossed to me with bowls and bracelets and skewers by the tribesmen of Dilfan, in Luristan, who had dug them out of graves; and I like to see them beside my silver with its Victorian chiselling, or to think, when Mlle. Claude brings Schiaparelli's newest fancies to be admired, of the carefully hammered loop which was sewn with feeling so similar on to the lost Sassanian garment. There is no end to the pleasure of objects if once one comes to see them as connected in this way. Some can be traced, like tobacco and the implements of smoking, through a known and recent history almost back to their origins: but even these have differentiated themselves as they scattered in the world, and the long-stemmed pipes of Kadhimain look exotic to an English eye, with little props round the bowls to hold them steady when tribesmen rest them on the floors of their tents as they sit.

Most objects go back much further and are lost to our memory, such as the patterns now woven in carpets of Anatolia, still to be recognized among Byzantine treasures threaded in silks or beaten in gold.

In Isfahan, among the gardens, a noble family lives in a country home on its own lands: round the estate the white-stemmed poplars make a thin noise like rain in the egg-shell sky of spring; and a stone's throw away, under pomegranates and a blossoming almond tree, a flat-roofed mud cottage houses the carpet-weavers who live and work, year in and year out, for the sons and daughters of the house. I was taken to see the loom on which a rug already showed islands of

63

colour; two girls were weaving there while a small brother, cross-legged below, helped with his tiny fingers, more agile than theirs; the work, they said, would take two years. The design was drawn for them, "but we scarcely need that," they said. "These are the patterns of our land; we learn them with our mothers' milk"; they are still the great arabesques and shields and stems and roses which one may find hung on the walls of museums all over the world. The man with the machine imitates them. "You can scarcely tell the difference," the poor fool says now and then: but the rather eccentric polygons he copies have no particular shaping in his heart; they are no longer the roses "transferred with our mothers' milk," grown strange but lovely through handling and time.

> Oh, no man knows
> Through what wild centuries
> Roves back the rose.*

Not the tongue, nor the mind—but the fingers know it, and the hearts of the weavers of Isfahan.

If this radical difference were remembered and respected there would be no harm in machine-made things; they have their own violent realms, their own flood-like beneficence; they are dangerous only when they think of themselves as substitutes for the other—so eliminating at once all those values which they can never share. Whether the hand or the engine has made them, the objects we use are the shuttles of our human design; as they come and go, the colour of life changes; and frontiers seem irrelevant when we think of the silk-worm carried from China, or the Swiss watch ticking through the world. Nothing indeed is sadder than the efforts now made by governments to build high dykes to dam this ceaseless ebb and flow; as if the departmental scissors were cutting the human body through all its little veins to separate the lungs and liver, the head and heart.

"We are extremely depressed by the fall of Paris," some ladies from Lhassa in Tibet remarked to a friend of mine in India. "It is where we bought all our cosmetics."

In the bazaar of Bagdad, swathed in her black cottons

* WALTER DE LA MARE.

64

roughened by the sun, a Beduin woman sat on the ground with her basket before her, stacked with a small array of pink chalk sticks with which to smear and beautify one's cheeks. "What do you call these in Arabic?" I asked her. "They are called *moda*," she replied—which is the Italian for fashion; in the sun-streaked bazaar she seemed to be sitting in the shadow of the Crusades.

Nationalism is a cutting and dividing virtue; people are frozen there in the shadow of collective adjectives, whose truth or falsehood is rarely brought home to them, and in any case seems remotely related to efforts of their own. But if one thing is more certain than another it is that the human soul is not collective; and the skeletons of Belsen show what happens when it tries to become so. The planner's shadow, perhaps efficient with external things, falls like death on the realms of the spirit where man the hand-made article, not mass-produced, stands on his feet alone.

A network of human relationships involves him, and the neglect and forgetfulness of these, and their substitution with collective bogies, have debased the individual image in our time. Those virtues which oblige us to lift the burdens of others—obedience and chastity for instance—have fallen almost into disrepute. They are dual virtues: when looked upon as personal, their certainties are blurred; they are duets in which two hearts must keep time, and the safety, the joy of one human being are given by them into the keeping of another. Human happiness is subtly dependent in their concord, and the whole welfare of man appears involved in the recognition of dependence while "every man for himself" takes us away from the very meaning of the world. For the drama of men is that their goodness creates, and their wickedness shatters, the goodness of others; so that pity holds us ever in leash, and there is no solitary road.

We set out, in the dawn of life gathering the tackle for our voyage, and soon leave the vessel of our elders and push our own craft to sea; and in strange ports gather new merchandise with opening eyes, and make with a steady or a wavering sail for the western stars: and on the high seas meet with traffickers and friends, and exchange our bales, and lift perhaps, to carry for someone in his shipwreck, the bundle of his treasure and his love. With our own goods we may traffic as we will; but what we take from another is dearer than our own, for we know not but it may be all the man has left him, and that his life may sink with it if we push it overboard; therefore we shall look carefully at what we take upon our decks, to see that it is indeed treasure and not nonsense, and—being sure of its value—carry it to the end.

For even if it is some trifle merely, that we cast in carelessness or wilfulness away, the little wraith that was offered to our keeping will raise its small drowned head and haunt us. One such memory comes to me now and then, and is still sharp in spite of time; and it seems a trifling matter. It happened in a small town of the Alps where much of our childhood was passed, and a company of travelling players came for a week or two, and put up a notice of *Hamlet* among their other bills. We went, my sister and I with my father, and it was a very poor, long-winded *Hamlet* in Italian, with not a word left out: the stage seemed very small, the players larger than life: the soliloquies more numerous than ever I remember: and in short, before it was half over, we got up in our very conspicuous box and left. We learned afterwards that the play had been put on particularly to please us; we were people of some small importance in that remote town and the players had found out that we were English; and their humiliation, so stupidly but unwittingly inflicted, still bites a little at my heart.

Nearly every life is haunted by such orphans, left upon its doorstep and allowed to die. But when one contemplates *intentional* cruelty, the deliberate horror of our world, no balm except oblivion can be imagined for him who with opened eyes may see the shipwrecks he has caused. And perhaps the Mercy for evil is annihilation, a painless ceasing from the causing of sorrow; and that is what the most wicked will most wish for if among all their wickedness a spark of good remain? For the consequences of evil acts live on, and that is the grief and sorrow of the world. And if human good survives and comprehends from timeless peace the mixture of its earthly being, and sees how the evil wrought by the evil that was in it works itself out with age-long continuance in time: then one can imagine that no wish remains to it except for evil itself to die and forget itself, in Mercy for those who

66

have forgotten mercy and are faced with the horror of the knowledge of themselves.

These are points far beyond the range of my short compass, and I return to the tangible things with which we started, pebbles on that shore of time above which the greater stars continually rise and set. The individual man builds his wares and practises his virtues and both of them are links inextricably twisted in a chain of personal bonds throughout the world. In their midst, and free in his fetters, the human creature answers for his soul, and the mass-produced collective is as useful for his service as the collective wheat is useful for his bread. Yet the reaper still reaps and the gatherer garners, and the woman shapes and cuts the loaf for every individual home: and the glory of our machinery is nothing but the dressing of a slave attendant on the hand-made private life.

9
THE ARTIST

For only out of solitude or strife
Are born the sons of valour and delight;
        ROY CAMPBELL. *Choosing a Mast.*

... he must go on unprotected that he may be constantly changed.
        GERALD HEARD. *The Source of Civilization.*

        Draw from the shapeless moment
        Such pattern as you can.
                EDNA ST. VINCENT MILLAY.

That thou might'st speak, when speech was fit, and do, when deeds were done.
                Chapman's *Iliad*, IX, 422.

        Though his bark cannot be lost,
        Yet it shall be tempest-tost.
                                Macbeth.

... the confused rumble of civilization is pleasant to his senses.
        GEORGE SANTAYANA. *Soliloquies in England.*

There would seem at first sight, to be no more in his words than in other words.   But they are words of enchantment ... all the burial places of the memory give up their dead. ... Like the dwelling-place of our infancy revisited in manhood, like the song of our country heard in a strange land, they produce upon us an effect wholly independent of their intrinsic value.
                MACAULAY: on Milton.

To maintain a faultless style under all circumstances was a rule of good breeding and a result of habit.
        BURCKHARDT. *Civilization of the Italian Renaissance.*

9. THE ARTIST

"I CANNOT praise a fugitive and cloistered virtue, un-exercised and unbreathed, that never sallies out and sees her adversary, but slinks out of the race, where that immortal garland is to be run for not without dust and heat."

"Among the numerous requisites that must concur to complete an author, few are of more importance than an early entrance into the living world."

These two quotations, from Milton and from Johnson, are in the main stream of our tradition, which flows like a river into industry and ploughland from its unseen source of snows. It broke into our centuries with this same gallant voice out of its Roman, Norse, Celtic and Saxon past, and broadened into a genial stream that laughs and falls and dances in the sun and slips through the shadows of its time with no despair-ing murmur. Its living surface reflects the country fields and the smooth beechwoods, and loses no gleam of sky between their sober shades; and scoops its pools under banks of pas-tures, where the elder-flower in June smells sweet, and cows with moist square muzzles stand hovered over by a skimming of flies like haloes in the evening light. The stream flows from Beowulf and Chaucer and Langland and Shakespeare in the meadows, and its darkest eddies still hold the amber of the turf of their native soil, and move singing over deeps or shallows with waters drawn from perennial springs. Nor is there yet any sign of weariness or lack of strong limbs wrestling in the flood.

But here and there, both now and in the past, a few swim-mers refuse the current and—thinking themselves perhaps beside an Indian stream—discover along its banks some hermit cave. There in congenial twilight they "slink out of the race" and sit, like images of Buddha, enlarged and unreal. From the reedy joss-sticks of devotees, incense to their own works rises in the dead air in a tenuous coil which every vivid breath sways and disturbs and breaks. Here, in sterility, they hope to bring forth what life alone, in its strong embrace, engenders; and in the time of our trouble close their ears even to the faint transmuted trans-Atlantic echo of our current, whose foaming barriers Milton and all those others never feared.

The clear-eyed young men who do the work and know it not, give them one glance of disdain and turn away; and we, the average who try to steer in the whirlpools, listen with surprise to the far Olympic voices when they pontificate on Art. For even Prometheus, who brought divine fire, came down and took the consequences among the sons of men. And though some may be kings of remoteness and true saints and hermits, we find when we look close that it is but cowardice in the greater number—and, having said so much, must look again to seek an explanation for the artist's cowardice, if not an excuse.

For it is his nature to avoid unpleasantness in a degree which to normal healthy people appears extreme, and to excuse it by explaining that things hurt him more than the uninitiate can understand. He is born and then trained to *feel* as a thoroughbred is born and trained to race—so that even joy, "das tiefe, schmerzensvolle glück,"* hurts him, and pain winds through his being like water through the arteries of the hills, wearing them away. If the production of great beauty were to be the guerdon of this heavy outlay, who would not gladly suffer? But the tragedy is that the money is paid down at the beginning and no one can tell, least of all the artist himself, whether the show that follows is worth looking at or no.

I often think of this when I watch a defeated face in some small orchestra, that grinds empty tunes among laughter and scraping of chairs and clink of tables in a place where music is forgotten; and I try to read, under the dull routine and set

* GOETHE. *Faust.*

crust of features, what dreams first ushered in the morning to that fat opaque man blowing his trombone, or to the nervous youth with shabby eyes who rests his violin so wearily upon his knee when the piece is finished and turns the pages of his music with such dead hands. They, too, must have started out with visions of obedient orchestras and lamplit applause; and listened to Ariel voices in the gossip of the air; until contact not with the real but with the bitter world of men, and their own weakly furnished spirits, flung them like economic driftwood on a bare shore. There, where all, with casual feet, may tread them under, their fragile soul retracts like a sea-creature on its rock when the wave washes out to the sea; and in their weakness they relinquish the artist's honour, the ornament which his own heart alone can buy—they relinquish as far as is in them their readiness to *feel*.

It is not the normal being, with seven fairly thick skins, who should condemn those with an epidermis missing when they shrink from the common touch or scuttle like crabs with uncovered backs in the blast of war, or build themselves a refuge of routine, or drink, or solitude, or dullness—anything which may produce a barrier between them and their too great sensitiveness to the impact of things. But let them keep quiet about it, and not touch themselves up as models, or rail against a world which—luckily, I suspect, in spite of all—is not built on a vacuum of renunciation. For the artist's business is to take sorrow when it comes. The depth and capacity of his reception is the measure of his art; and when he turns his back on his own suffering, he denies the very laws of his being and closes the door on everything that can ever make him great.

People have retired to more quiet and prosperous continents to keep the instrument of their utterance unstained and fresh: as if the owners of motor-cars should hoist them up in air, where the wheels turn swift and smooth, clear of the dust and grinding surfaces of highways. They get nowhere —for the paths of our journeys must still be the paths of men: and our leaders and companions are those who walk with us, and find their own rewards in wayside shades and quiet pauses, not unforgetful of the journey's end.

As I am writing this I come upon a review of the new

manuscript of Malory, whom Mr. Rouse describes as "another Warwickshire man."

"Of an old family of small gentry, he was a follower of Warwick the Kingmaker, involved in his shifting and devious policies, caught in the disasters of the Wars of the Roses. After a respectable beginning, suddenly in the course of the years 1450–51, he is charged with several major crimes, robbery, theft, cattle raids, breaking into a monastery, rape and laying an ambush to murder the Duke of Buckingham. . . . There is no longer any doubt that this is the man who wrote the immortal tales. He wrote them in prison, and several of the colophons that Caxton omitted are prayers for the knight-prisoner's speedy deliverance. . . . The tales reflect the disorder, the distraction of Malory's own time: the unity and triumph of Henry V's reign broken down into the fratricidal strife, the conflicts of loyalties, the murderousness and wretchedness of the Wars of the Roses. It is all faithfully reflected in Malory's wonderful books: the break-up of the unity of the Round Table, of the purpose and prosperity of Arthur's early reign, the growth of disunion and disloyalty, brother against brother, the guilt of the Queen, the gathering ominousness of the civil war between Arthur and his nephew Mordred, the tragic end" (*Sunday Times*, June 22, 1947).

"Then were they condescended" [Malory writes] "that King Arthur and Sir Mordred should meet betwixt both their hosts, and every each of them should bring fourteen persons; and they came with this word unto Arthur. Then said he: I am glad that this is done: and so he went into the field. And when Arthur should depart, he warned all his host that an they see any sword drawn: Look ye come on fiercely, and slay that traitor, Sir Mordred, for I in no wise trust him. In likewise Sir Mordred warned his host that: An ye see any sword drawn, look that ye come on fiercely, and so slay all that ever before you standeth; for in no wise I will not trust for this treaty, for I know well my father will be avenged on me. And so they met as their appointment was, and so they were agreed and accorded thoroughly; and wine was fetched, and they drank. Right soon came an adder out of a little heath bush, and it stung a knight on the foot. And when the knight felt him stung, he looked down and saw the adder, and then he drew his sword to slay the adder, and thought of none other harm. And when the host on both parties saw that sword drawn, then they blew beamous, trumpets, and horns, and shouted grimly. And so both hosts dressed them together. And King Arthur took his horse, and said: Alas this unhappy day! and so rode to his party. And Sir Mordred in likewise."

Terrible or tragic history is not necessary for the production of greatness in art; the faintest summer breath holds melodies and dirges enough if genius happens to be listening. But results even then are in close relation to the weight of the feeling behind them, and it is possible that people are searched more deeply, the surface of life is pierced more frequently, and the stimulus is sharper in an age of conflict, than in those periods which we fallaciously think of as secure. Nothing here is secure, and in this certainty the future of art lies safe. A sense of tremendous mortal vicissitude looms behind

> The expense of spirit in a waste of shame,"*

or Raleigh:

> Even such is Time, that takes in trust
> Our youth, our joys, our all we have,

or Herbert:

> Sweet day, so cool, so calm, so bright!

The brittle quality shines in every work of art that has in it the elements of greatness.

I have often thought that the fatalism of the Muslim faith has taken the edge off Arabic poetry, so that one must go to Persian mystics or to the Pagans of the days before Muhammad to hear the heart speak: for fatalism too is a device by which, in a hard Oriental world, the human creature barricades and protects its own defencelessness of feeling.

* SHAKESPEARE. Sonnet.

75

In the West, and with our greatest such as Shakespeare, the answer is not to renounce, but to endure. In the climax of the great tragedies, both Edgar and Hamlet reach the conviction that ripeness or readiness is all. In these plays Shakespeare poses the riddle of suffering, the slight, unnoticed cause, the terrible reply.

> As flies to wanton boys, are we to the gods;
> They kill us for their sport.*

Gloucester says it, who has done no evil except in the one short passage of his youth, who has offered fate nothing but loyalty free from pride or anger, and yet falls into the bitterness of grief as deeply as Lear himself. Edgar speaks the words which are man's answer and victory:

> What, in ill thoughts again? Men must endure
> Their going hence, even as their coming hither:
> Ripeness is all:

and again:

> GLOUCESTER: . . . henceforth I'll bear
> Affliction till it do cry out itself
> 'Enough, enough' and die. . . .
> EDGAR: Bear free and patient thoughts. . . .

He describes himself as:

> A most poor man, made tame to fortune's blows;
> Who, by the art of known and feeling sorrows,
> Am pregnant to good pity.

Man conquers by enduring. Over and over again the poet says so in these later plays in which one feels in every line a hammer stroke as it were on his heart: and even in earlier ones like *Richard II* which are forerunners:

> . . . woe doth the heavier sit,
> Where it perceives it is but faintly borne

* *King Lear.*

For gnarling sorrow hath less power to bite
The man that mocks at it, and sets it light.

BRUTUS: O, that a man might know
The end of this day's business, ere it come!
But it sufficeth, that the day will end,
And then the end is known.

ANTONY: Nay, good my fellows, do not please sharp fate
To grace it with your sorrows: bid that welcome
Which comes to punish us, and we punish it
Seeming to bear it lightly.

TIMON: . . . my long sickness
Of health and living now begins to mend,
And nothing brings me all things.

and:

1ST SENATOR: He's truly valiant that can wisely suffer
The worst that man can breathe, and make his wrongs
His outsides, to wear them like his raiment, carelessly,
And ne'er prefer his injuries to his heart,
To bring it into danger.

and again Timon:

To revenge is no valour, but to bear.

NESTOR: In the reproof of chance
Lies the true proof of men . . .
          . . . the thing of courage
As roused with rage with rage doth sympathize,
And with an accent tun'd in selfsame key
Retorts to chiding fortune.

HAMLET: If it be now, 'tis not to come; if it be not to come,
it will be now; if it be not now, yet it will come: the readiness is all;

In *Hamlet* it seems clear that Shakespeare comes to his
conclusion, and the crime and its revenge are not the central
problem. The great soliloquy puts the question—whether

it is better to endure or to act—the question of Martha or Mary, one of the decisive questions of the world.

From the time of that soliloquy, Hamlet's adversary is not Claudius, but the whole unmerited transitory nature of things that come to attack the human spirit. This attack is shown again and again—the faithlessness of friends, the frailty of love, the passing away of even the features of those once known. The grave-scene is the climax, the last example of the unreliability of all: and Hamlet's philosophy here is contrasted with that of Laertes, the man of action, who is so swift to revenge his father's and sister's death, who is what the ghost asked Hamlet to be and what Hamlet—having paused and pondered—rejected.

It seems to me that a point that is overlooked in the judging of Hamlet is the fact that the ghost and his advice come up from "sulphurous and tormenting flames," so that the wisdom of the advice is not to be assumed: the ghost's voice is not so very far removed from the voices that misled Macbeth. The contrast between Hamlet and Laertes is surely in Hamlet's favour. When he returns a changed man from his journey, he has answered his question: he knows that it matters little whether he kills Claudius or no: his fury in the struggle at the grave's edge is against the shallowness of action: and the words he says—"I loved Ophelia"—are the most eloquent, the most poignant measure of the suffering that brought him through things temporal to things eternal. The last great clue comes just before the fencing match: *the readiness is all*; and after that the death of Hamlet and the King are minor matters, to Hamlet himself and to his author.

By endurance the garland is won; "not without dust and heat." It is the same human garland for all; but the artist, the most delicate of our instruments for joy or sorrow, endures more than others: like the mermaid in Hans Andersen's tale, he dances before his love with swords in his feet; and the pain becomes unbearable if the things he suffers for and moves among are not immortal.

10

STYLE

Thus ornament is but the guilèd shore
To a most dangerous sea.

Merchant of Venice.

She was not a woman of many words; for, unlike people in general, she proportioned them to the number of her ideas.

JANE AUSTEN. *Sense and Sensibility.*

Poetry is nothing less than the most perfect speech of man, that in which he comes nearest to being able to utter the truth.

MATTHEW ARNOLD. Preface to Wordsworth's poems.

Il faut être léger pour voler à travers les âges.

ANATOLE FRANCE. *Vie Litt.*, II.

SOCRATES: How real existence is to be studied or discovered is, I suspect, beyond you and me. But we may admit so much, that the knowledge of things is not to be derived from names. No, they must be studied and investigated in themselves.

PLATO. *Cratylus.*

L'art d'ennuyer est de tout dire.

. . . for the letter killeth but the spirit giveth life.

First Epistle of Paul to the Corinthians, iii. 6.

. . . in literature as in the plastic arts and in life itself, the nude is nearer to virtue than the décolleté.

HAVELOCK ELLIS. *Affirmations.*

10. STYLE

IT is not for nothing that of the two most beautiful tombs of the Italian Renaissance one lies in Ravenna. In spite of improved health with diminished malaria; of an atmosphere of agricultural prosperity, busy with dog-carts and bicycles on market days; of the rich increase of tillage as swamps are drained and the long flat aisles of the pines are cut; in spite of all this there is still an atmosphere of death over Ravenna. This often belongs to places stranded and abandoned by the sea; and in Ravenna there was another flood, that ebbed as it gathered to Byzantium from the west. The air of the deserted empire lingers round baptismal domes and unfrequented basilicas; its cold light shines on innocent emblems of a Christian faith long separated from us by youth and time, and on fantasies more ancient, though nearer to us in their sophistication, that shine in the untarnished shimmer of mosaics, like motionless pools filled with ocean gardens left by a receding tide.

Amid all these phantoms, the group that holds me longest is that of the Empress Theodora among her ladies in San Vitale. There is here an exquisite finish, as of an art that has reached its very limit of perfection; it tells the tale of the civilization it belongs to as Flecker's statue was to tell its message with beautiful hands. The figures stand round the crowned dancing girl in a formal group, full of courtly awareness, neither pressing nor yielding, and the artist—practised in the world's way—has given care to the gorgeous detail of each garment, to the collars of threaded gems, to the expensive veil that lies upon the wrist with such accomplished lightness, to the badges of rank—strange lozenge patches—

81

laid on the long mantles of the nobles. In every fold of the elaborate straight gowns, in the cold breeding of the eyes and hands and their languid treacherous repose, in the air of easy courtier respect that surrounds the empress who smoulders wilful and dangerous, encrusted with jewels and gold; in that lady-in-waiting, subservient and arrogant, so exquisitely maided, so cruelly sure of power—there is as it were a heightening of meaning, an electric charge of something that the actual ingredients of the picture are in themselves insufficient to explain.

It seems to me that one might define this heightening of meaning as *style*.

Style is fundamentally a truthful statement, if we take for truth something more careful than the not telling of a lie. There are layers and layers of truth; and style, whether in dress or life, art or literature, is involved in their discovery.

In the matter of dress, for instance, how profoundly justified is the scorn that every wise woman feels for the word "utility" and all that it implies. Utility, like charity, is not puffed up; it vaunteth not itself; it is comparatively innocent, and does not make of its victims aliens to their own selves, which is active falsehood and bad taste and a pitfall to the unwary who think expense and fashion are enough. Utility is not unseemly. But it seeks to avoid offence in a dull, negative way by discovering an average in human needs and the average is dowdy. Now truth is *never* average. Since there is not one single thing in the world exactly like another, the very essence of truth is that it leaps across averages to the particular, at any rate as far as anything is concerned that we are likely to have to deal with on this earth: and therefore Woman, who is primitive and deals with ultimate facts, will do the best she can to particularize her utility into some trick, some shape, some detail, which fits her own surroundings and herself. To her men she appears infatuated by singularity—and we may admit that there are moments of excess—but at her best it is herself that she is trying to discover; and if she or her dressmaker succeed, she achieves the secret of style in her clothes.

The art of life is no different, and the integrity of the individual with himself gives him that quality of style which we call breeding, whether he be a herdsman or a king. In the whole realm of art and literature this foundation of sincerity is the beginning if not the end of *style*.

In a night of the month of April, the Arabs say that the oysters rise from their beds and float on the surface of the sea; and open their ragged shaly lips to collect a dew-drop as it falls; and so, having been united with heaven, descend again; and in the dim opaque twilight of their existence work their pearl round the heavenly core and build it with shining skins of light, one upon the other immeasurably fine, which the merchant later peels off at his pleasure, and stops where he pleases, when he is satisfied with the sheen of his jewel: for to that central dew-drop, invisible to men, no creature engaged in earthly commerce need trouble to attain. But the pearl will be more or less valuable according to the merchant's peeling, and he will hold it up for pleasure in his long slim Arab hand and wrap it in a shred of red velvet and bear it in his bosom, until he finds someone to buy it and carry it abroad, and hang it perhaps round the neck of folly, or possibly in the ear of kings.

So the artist treats the pearl of his life, penetrating as far as he may; and the infinite number of these layers, allowing for every variety of depth and surface, makes for the pleasant diversities of truth and style. For some will cut very deep on the shaft of a single emotion, like those who wrote epitaphs for the Greeks, or Bunyan in the *Pilgrim's Progress*; and some will throw a wide net and gather their style and truth out of the surface mixture of the world. To the stuff so gathered they must bring an ear and eye for harmony, in whatever their medium may be—but whether in the Divine Comedy, or the gay baroque of gardens, the qualities that make for style seem to me to be the same, and are perhaps outlined by Dr. Johnson when he says of Shakespeare that: "His descriptions have always some peculiarities, gathered by contemplating things as they really exist."

Dr. Livingstone, in his book on *The Greek Genius and its Meaning to Us*, draws a comparison between their classical treatment of the external world and that of Mrs. Robert Browning who, in one of her poems, describes a seagull's sentiments exactly like her own; the Greek, Dr. Livingstone rightly observes, would have presented the bird as he saw it and said no more.

He does not tell us why the Greek would treat the seagull with such restraint; but I think myself that it is because of a constant awareness in him of the small divinity of common objects, his vision of nymphs and dryads in every grove. In this is an origin of respect for the essence of things and reluctance to impinge upon their freedom, just as the modern awareness of the free soul in childhood has created a reluctance to twist it from its natural way. Even now, perhaps from association, or perhaps from the indelible enchantment of the land, this feeling holds like a charm as one walks in the mountains of Arcadia. Those cradled paths surrounded by so rich a solitude; the steep clear woods in the eagle-haunted air; the supple waters flowing in valleys where plane trees bathe their roots; the maiden-haired cups of waters in the hills—a sense of *independent* life is there, which one's own coming and going does not ruffle, a happy companionship of separate equality between the wanderer and the things he sees. I remember feeling like this on a radiant rain-washed morning as I turned a sudden corner and faced the pale sheet of the Stymphalian lake below. Sunlight lay above it as if the very air had turned to gold; and the voices of the frogs rose in a vast chorus, beaten like brass against the echoes of the hills, with a loud triumphant deafening affirmation that their universe was as free, urgent and important as that of the casual traveller, man.

The Greeks clearly felt this about the external world. In their respect for the integrity of things, they discovered a love of truth apart from human deviation. In the union of these two feelings they laid hold on the elusive immortality of diction.

All greatness in style begins, I imagine, with such respect, deep and passionate enough to produce a humility which will not assert itself at the expense even of inanimate things: out of which submissiveness a desire to serve is born, in disinterested accuracy towards the object, whatever it may be. If the first respect is lacking, the rest is but a façade with no building behind it; or if passion is not strong enough to sustain its service, no greatness can follow: but if both are there, the grace of style will be added "like wings to the feet of a bird," whether in art, philosophy or life.

This explains, I think, the diversity, and also the frequent un-selfconsciousness of style. The wayside ballads, Sir Patrick Spens and the Sisters of Binnorie, the Psalms, the Chronicles, the peasant songs of Sicily, or Roland with his Peers—are at one with the most sophisticated, with Theocritus, or Sir Osbert Sitwell, or Jane Austen, in the respect with which they approach their object and, knowingly or unknowingly, try to preserve its integrity as a gardener admits for each flower its separate aspect and soil. And this, I imagine, is why Dr. Livingstone selected Mrs. Browning's seagull for his contrast with the Greek verity, since the attribution of qualities, when they are arbitrary and foreign, is an infringement of those profound liberties which all men, and artists particularly, may feel in the surrounding world.

11

WORDS

. . . for we have discovered that names have by nature a truth, and that not every man knows how to give a thing a name.

PLATO. *Cratylus.*

O my good lord! the world is but a word.

Timon of Athens.

Look you, the worm is not to be trusted but in the keeping of wise people; for, indeed, there is no goodness in the worm.

Antony and Cleopatra.

Yea, words which are our subtlest and delicatest outward creatures, being composed of thoughts and breath, are so muddy and thick, that our thoughts themselves are so, because (except at the first rising) they are leavened with passions and affections.

DONNE.

La conversation de Charles était plate comme un trottoir de rue et les idées de tout le monde y défilaient, dans leur costume ordinaire.

FLAUBERT. *Madame Bovary.*

Thamus replied . . . this discovery of yours will create forgetfulness in the learners' souls, because they will not use their memories: they will trust to the external written characters and not remember of themselves. The specific which you have discovered is an aid not to memory, but to reminiscence, and you give your disciples not truth, but only the semblance of truth; they will be hearers of many things and will have learned nothing; they will appear to be omniscient and will generally know nothing; they will be tiresome company, having the show of wisdom without the reality.

PLATO. *Phaedrus.*

Where are now the warring kings
Word be-mockers?

W. YEATS. *The Song of the Happy Shepherds.*

II. WORDS

THE country about Asolo produces silk in quantity, and
long straight avenues of mulberry trees, pollarded to
a monotonous cabbage roundness, intersect the plain
and feed the silk grubs in their season. These are hatched
from small eggs like the heads of white and yellow pins, and
are kept on shallow trays in a moist warm atmosphere, eating
continually; until they grow to the size of a baby's finger,
grey and flabby as dead flesh, with soft twigs of legs and horns.
The worms eat day and night. Nothing but the mulberry
leaf will content them; and in a year when late seasons or
other disasters overtake their trees, they, like the poor people
of Bengal, die rather than change their diet. Ordinarily,
however, they munch busily for several weeks, until a collective idea drives them to climb from their pastures into
faggots of sticks which the peasants keep ready, where they
spin their cocoons and sleep. I have often seen them in all
these stages, and later also, when the cocoon dances in boiling
water and the thin spun thread is unwound from its packed
maze, and eventually lies in coils of hard yellow silk—moth
wings which will never fly; for the grub has been boiled
to death, and the heaps of carnage become the best of all
manures for roses, and are sold for a good price.

The peasants have little to do with the later stages for they
pull the cocoons out of their faggots and put them in sacks
and sell them; but while the grubs are still growing, they have
required sleepless attention and have been supplied constantly with sacks of the heart-shaped leaves. These they
instantly submerge in their crawling numbers, and devour.
In a great farm, I have seen a row of long rooms, opening

89

one from the other, filled with the restless shallow trays, so that all the air seemed to shimmer with a blind movement, as if molecules of formless matter had become visible. There is something obscene in almost any promiscuous heap: one's instinct thinks of it as dead rather than alive: and it causes uneasiness to see it moving, blind, anarchic, inspired by greed pure and simple, without a touch of any nobler pleasure.

Sometimes, out of a pile of these feeders, a little grey body lifts itself and waves blunt head and needy helpless arms in air: it is only asking more mulberry leaf of the invisible gods and is soon prone again and glued to the business of mastication. And if one listens, a terrifying noise like a smooth tide over shingle becomes audible—the grinding of the small innumerable jaws.

I sometimes think that words are like those feeders, biting their way into the substance of our lives. Obscure and neutral in themselves, we shuffle them and throw to them not only the thoughts of our mind and the feelings of our heart—their proper diet—but any refuse of imitation that comes to hand; for, unlike the silkworm, the word-grub will accept promiscuous garbage for his food. Yet he can produce the fine and shining thread which makes our kingly garments; and he, too, waking from sleep, can grow wings, like that creature in whose brightness the Greek poets recognized the soul. And at any moment, if we listen, we can hear the sound of the minute teeth of the sleepless words lisping or hissing, soothing or menacing, biting into the lives of men.

Nothing to-day is more ominous than our disregard of these small dangerous slaves. They are being used as it were to corrupt themselves. And we are coming to forget that they, who in themselves are nothing but emptiness and air, must embody other, more solid things—justice, for instance—whose very existence depends on an awareness of exactitude in words.

"This would be a very quiet world if those who had nothing to say—said it." The notice was put up, pathetically, in an American business man's office.

One of the pleasant things among the Arabs is their recognition of silence as a part of human intercourse: they sit round in a large gathering and, when the formal greetings and enquiries after health or absent friends are over, they let the minutes pass, two, four, ten minutes, in meditation, until someone takes an idea and throws it like a stone into the middle of a pond, where all have time to watch its ripples spread. Perhaps one must have country memories to fall easily into this way. I can recall days with my father or my godfather—both lovers of walking and hills. We would step side by side or—on narrow paths—one behind the other for many hours, and talk would come to the surface and die, easily, with long gaps, like those underground rivers whose course is shown by occasional stretches that vanish again among the stones. The landscape would seem to take a part in this conversation, washing into its pauses with changing views and the shadows of travelling clouds and westering light; so that the things one said or heard came to be like small jewels set in their twist of hours, made permanent by the frame into which they fell. Ever since these days I have thought that the luxury of conversation is to hold it in such surroundings as may enrich its pauses, and have wondered whether the British taciturnity is not responsible in some measure for the care we take of our homes by comparison with more talkative races, making them pleasant places for words to drift into silence.

"As all suns pass before the face of darkness, and hide it awhile with their splendour, so on many-coloured wings thought flies through the silence, but the silence endures."*

Built up into the pauses of Time words sparkle more brightly, like necklaces set on black velvet. And with so advantageous a background it becomes a matter of importance that the gems should be real.

But we seem to have forgotten the dignity of the only instruments, among all our inventions, that can carry and make articulate the thoughts, the soul of man. Even when used without so high an intention, words may yet be innocent and make a pleasant noise in the world, like brooks on moss and stones, or the wind in the trees. But their *misuse* perverts the divine. And we have now come to a pass where truthlessness is tolerated, and even expected,

* GEORGE SANTAYANA. *Dialogues in Limbo.*

in politics, diplomacy, advertisement, the education of children
and the privacy of marriage.   The depth of our degradation
of words may be measured by the surprise any newspaper
editor would feel if his news were criticized merely for being
untrue.

A good deal of this comes, I believe, from dullness and
the notion that truth is indivisible and single.   We are apt
to think of virtue as monotony and to allow all the graces
of variety to the other side.   As a matter of fact nothing is
more capricious than accuracy, nor more elusive, nor more
difficult to hold when caught; for every word is blurred to
begin with by being moulded twice over in different moulds
—first in the mind of the speaker and then in that of the listener
—so that even with every precaution it can never do more
than be approximate to the object of which it speaks.

Anyone who tries to write knows that there is not the
simplest most tangible thing in existence that can be described
entire.   The roots of all go down uncharted, like sea rocks
whose wizened surface the smallest waves lick over—though
great mountains and submarine valleys may underlie them,
with monsters or mermaids in their depths.   All this and more,
to the very centre of earth and extremity of time, is part of
their truth; and the task of every statement or description
is to decide how much of it all is to be included.

As a rule, we are satisfied with a surface verity and say
of these rocks that they are bleached or dry or sharp or
rounded, ignoring and even contradicting the foundations
on which they stand: but those who possess the secret of words
are able as it were to pack the meaning, and fill it with greater
space and wider time, so that a more capacious quality of
truth is implicit in the things they say.   Shakespeare does
this constantly with the use of images and comparisons which
he compresses until they fuse, so that only the surface point
of a noun or verb or adjective is left to show what range of
country lies submerged below.

Any number of such single, revealing words can be collected in any one of the plays.

In *Timon of Athens*:

> all kind of natures
> That labour on the *bosom* of this sphere.

Bowing his head against the steepy mount
To *climb* his *happiness.*

My uses *cry* to me.

Our vaults have *wept*
With drunken spilth of wine.

If I would *broach* the *vessels* of my love.

LUCIUS' SERVANT: What do you think the hour?
PHILOTUS: *Labouring* for nine.

Convert, o' the instant, green *virginity.*

like Juliet's "Bloody Tybalt, yet but *green* in earth."

Every one of these words is a compression of two images,
and could be a detailed simile or metaphor such as:

Thou art a slave, whom Fortune's tender arm
With favour never clasp'd; but bred a dog.

which might easily have been: "Thou art Fortune's dog," if
Shakespeare, hurrying on as usual, had left us to reconstruct
the rest. I think that the delight which moves across his
pages is very largely due to these signposts, which he scatters
with careless prodigality to be deciphered and followed by
readers as they can. Each of them owes its value to the
accuracy of the resemblance which first inspired the image of
which the one intrusive word remains; the word itself is
solitary and swift as a fork of lightning, but it lifts out of darkness a landscape which the reader may recognize.

Yet neither Shakespeare nor any other magician can ever
utter the whole truth, or even express what he really means to
say. This penalty was laid on human speech when or before
the tower of Babel stood: perhaps it produced the germ of
discontent in Eden. Every later revolution in history is
the record of human efforts to keep words and their meaning
as nearly together as they can, for the quality of civilization

depends on the calling of things by their proper names as far as we can know them. It is the endless quest and the nations that turn from it totter and fall. Therefore with no idle misgiving we now watch governments build with useless words, and meet and part again with their fallacious hope that the nature of things has been altered when they find different epithets to call them by. I once heard of a little Arab boy whose parents familiarly referred to him as "Puncture," so that by the lowly disguise—the most depressing they could think of—the celestial envy might be disarmed. Our official spokesmen have less humility, but the process is often the same.

To cherish words is, it seems to me, the only safety. The love of them is natural to children, so that they can be fostered and by many arts be made allies of truth though imperfect, until they come to be chosen as carefully as one would choose a walking-stick, smooth and strong and free of knots, to bear without breaking the weight of the deeds that lean upon them.

12

GIVING AND RECEIVING

In this, my debt, I seem'd loath to confesse,
In that, I seem'd to shunn beholdingnesse.

    DONNE. *To the Countess of Bedford.*

My heartlet: God from Heaven, He is the thatcher who
 hath thatched it.
A house wherein wet rain pours not, a place wherein thou
 fearest not spear points;
Bright as though in a garden, and it without a fence round
 it.

  REICHENAU, in Helen Waddell. *The Wandering Scholars.*

        he would a traveller pray
To be his guest, his friendly house stood in the broad high-
 way,
In which he all sorts nobly us'd.

      Chapman's *Iliad*, VI, 15.

Ill fares the land, to hast'ning ills a prey,
Where wealth accumulates, and men decay;

   OLIVER GOLDSMITH. *The Deserted Village.*

. . . that species of courteous reserve and attention to the
wants of others, which is often found in primitive nations,
especially such as are always in arms; because a general
observance of the rules of courtesy is necessary to prevent
quarrels, bloodshed, and death.

   WALTER SCOTT. *The Fair Maid of Perth.*

If you accept them, then their worth is great.

    Taming of the Shrew.

12. GIVING AND RECEIVING

IF I had to beg for my living I would rather do so in Asia than in Europe or America; not that Asiatic poverty is in itself more tolerable, but because they give a moral status to beggary there which the Reformation, or the Industrial Revolution, has long ago destroyed with us. The beggar in Asia, if the West has not yet touched him, comes up with no whine of servility; his "looped and windowed raggedness" is no stock-in-trade to awaken compassion, but is worn naturally; his hand is held out in a gesture of giving almost more than receiving; and when you have handed your coin, he refers you to Allah: "Allah will repay," as a young woman buying a hat might tell them to send the bill to her husband.

This is all a result of the acknowledged certainty that, whatever the beggar's own moralities may be, he is the cause of virtue in others. As he lays his stick and the out-trodden remnants of his sandals beside him and squats, impregnated to the very soul one would think with the dust which has soaked him to one colour, so that his nakedness and the frayed bits of things that hang about it seem all one—as he unties the small round lump in his clothes where his takings are stored— he can be satisfied to think that every one of the collected coins has been a stepping-stone towards heaven for some good person's feet.

This sort of feeling must have existed in Europe before the Reformation and the Old Testament put virtue and property on one pedestal together. I used to meet it when I began to learn Arabic in San Remo. An old Francisan missionary whose white beard reached his girdle and who lived in a monastery on the hill, taught me. My lesson with him meant

97

a pilgrimage twice a week in the hottest part of the day, beginning with an hour's walk along the coast in dust and shadow under olive trees; then half an hour with my sand-wiches to eat in a train crowded with market women and large open baskets of carnations; and then I would turn away from the main street of San Remo and the Casino and the tourists and expensive Riviera shops, and find a climbing alley that led to the monastery door.

Here the beggars collected, sitting on the warm sloping pavement in the shade—old people nearly all of them, or idiots—each with a bowl or pipkin ready for food in their hand. I came to know them quite well, and to think of them as a sort of club, or the potter's shop in Fitzgerald's quatrains, with the brown-robed monk and his bucket of soup in the opening door as the crescent moon they were all waiting for. But there was an undercurrent of malevolence, and one felt that a misery to one might be greeted with a cackle of joy by all the rest. And there was a slight oppres-sion about the distribution of the food, a taint of philanthropy—though almost imperceptible—as if in the good steam of rice, beans, radishes and tomatoes that rose from the bucket there were a whiff of sensible and appetising grossness to mark the subtle barrier which divides givers and receivers.

The whole business of giving and receiving, it seems to me, should be lifted from the confines of duty into those of pleasure. Happiness is loving and making, and ends in gifts as naturally as the stem of a plant ends in a flower. A gift that is given out of a sense of duty is spoilt and, I believe, does harm.

How we hate the domestic martyr who, with a face of suffering, busies herself with disagreeable things we ought perhaps to be doing ourselves. It is worse when he or she (usually she) must do even those things that she likes to do with a laborious machinery of duty, saying to herself that there is an Ought about it. My mother had a friend of this sort, a woman who became embittered in her later years and would say harsh unmeaning things until, wracked by repent-ance, she rushed away to buy some object for the injured one who naturally received it surlily enough. One lived with her in a tiresome alternation of being prodded and soothed until, like a sea-anemone poked at with a stick one closed up

98

altogether. She could never accept invitations, which she loved, without saying: "I think So-and-so might feel hurt if I did not go." And at her dinners, which were good, she would lean over to say how she herself had walked in heat, or rain or whatever was unwelcome, to choose the fish, or strawberries, or pheasant; so that one could not enjoy even those few mouthfuls without feeling that they had cost trouble and discomfort to come by.

The true giver gathers bounty and sheds it, knowing that it is but a part of what he and all men receive all the time.

Desert Arabs understand this subtlety, and their readiness to give and take is one of the pleasant things about their code of values. If you visit a poor tent where you are expected, so that a sheep has been killed for your arrival and out in the scrub among the thorns there is a coming and going of women about the fire and the biggest of the copper trays are scoured and the mats or dyed gazelle skins are laid out on the sandy floor, you will do well if, unobtrusively as you enter, you lean a bag of rice or flour, and perhaps a smaller one of coffee or sugar, against the post of the tent; for this does not infringe the laws of hospitality and makes it possible for your host to offer happily what he has, with no aftermath of starvation for himself. Not that he would behave differently if the rite were omitted, for the honour of hospitality is so great that a desert man will sacrifice the last of what he has without showing his anxiety. I once discussed this with two young effendis from Damascus. They happened to be crossing the desert with me in the same car, and turned away from a group of Anezah camel youths who came to ask for water while we changed a tyre. The young townsmen evidently thought themselves creatures of a different kind from the poor rough people blackened by the sun, who would give their last drop to any thirsty traveller when he asked for it. They watched me in silence, completely unconvinced, as I handed my water-bottle to the half-clad lads; and these drank with their easy freedom and spoke to me as to an equal, and with a turn of their shoulders, quite unconscious, exiled the car and its inhabitants to the inanimate surrounding landscape incapable of human interchange. They had been four days out with their camels, away from the tents of their tribe.

It would be interesting to discover where the sense of property wakens and makes the giving of gifts possible. A cat will bring its mouse or dead lizard to lay as a trophy at the feet of its friends, and there is no doubt that a dog is possessive about his bone. In the jungles of south India live the Bhils, who are said to have been there before the last ice age pushed a wedge into anthropology. You can see them hovering, rather remote and bewildered, at any wayside station as you travel to cantonments in Bangalore or anywhere where there is jungle near, south to Travancore or north into Rajputana. They look quite different from all the races that followed them—small, gay, elusive, and indeed what they are, wild creatures of their woods; and when they range about in their own homes, before civilization has touched them, I am told that they will give away anything they have for the mere asking, and know neither avarice nor envy. For they look upon objects as we look upon air and sunlight and the other free gifts of God.

After this stage of the world as it must have been before and soon after the coming of man, when "Non rastros patietur humus, non vinea falcem,"* the long ladder of possessiveness begins. It climbs through family, tribe, sect and nation, obtaining gifts heroic and enduring, but tainted by limitation, which makes them into effigies or extensions of the giver's self, as if one attempted to acquire merit by endowing one's own scarecrow with one's own garments. Nepotism, for instance, is one of these, and looks white or black according as you see it with Eastern or Western eyes; for the Oriental will support all his relations with uncomplaining abnegation, and will promote, with a quiet mind and generally at the government's expense, the welfare of all his kindred and treat as a simple duty of generosity what the West looks upon as a selfish extension of family influence for personal ends. Either interpretation may be true, and it is not safe to generalize.

There are pitfalls, therefore, in the giving of gifts and, if one is in doubt about it, it is perhaps better to stick to the part of the receiver which in itself embraces most of the

* VIRGIL. *Eclogue IV.*

art of life. There is no doubt that the good receiver is
nearer to God. His heart is open, a great uncurtained unfurnished room where the obstacles of his own bric-à-brac
are not always in the way, and the days and nights can throw
their shadows as they pass. There is generosity in giving,
but gentleness in receiving.

Of this art the Arabs know little. They take a gift and,
with one swift appraising glance, put it aside, nor ever refer
to it again; so that there is only a shade or so in general behaviour to tell whether they are pleased or no. The common
emphasis on giving has indeed helped to destroy the receptive
attitude in us all. Yet the one is but a personal luxury, a
thing to be earned and worked for, an extra, a garland for
one's own head at the feast of life: the other is a part of that
general thankfulness which is worked into the very dough
of which our bread is kneaded—it comes with every day of
sunshine or night of stars: and gratitude is the greatest
tribute which one human being can offer to another, since
it is the same as must be offered with every breath of our
happiness to God.

We feel this unconsciously, and love those people who give
with humility, or who accept with ease.

The rich start with a background of property marked
"Private," and are handicapped as givers. They forget that
there are no possessions great enough to turn one from a
debtor to a creditor in this world; the very beginning of
gifts is the knowledge that all is one vast store, of which it is
pleasant to hand something on, a cupful out of a flowing
stream. They are apt to forget too that the tangible gifts
are the smallest part of the store of human treasure. Beyond
the enclosed reaches, the true giver comes again into the virgin
forest of the Bhils, beside those rivers where use and need may
dip: where receiving and giving are parts of a single action,
a loveliness that grows like lilies in the coolness of a glade
and, drawing all influences into its shining buds, scatters
without effort the sweetness by which it lives.

13
WOMEN'S EDUCATION

Uneducated clever women, who have seen much of the world, are in middle life so much the most cultured part of the community. They have been saved from this horrible burden of inert ideas.

PROF. WHITEHEAD. *The Aims of Education.*

Admonish your wives with kindness, because women were created from a crooked bone of the side; therefore if you wish to straighten it, you will break it, and if you let it alone, it will always be crooked.

MISHKAT. *Bab al-Nikah.*

. . . for myself I prayed for wealth, honour, and friends, for her (his wife) blamelessness, honesty, and that she might be a good housekeeper.

Agnolo Pandolfini in Burckhardt's *Civilization of the Italian Renaissance.*

British Liberalism has been particularly cruel to love; in the Victorian era all its amiable impulses were reputed indecent, until a marriage certificate suddenly rendered them godly, though still unmentionable.

GEORGE SANTAYANA. *Soliloquies in England.*

. . . to him that should extinguish the tapers of a lighthouse, might justly be imputed the calamities of shipwrecks.

SAMUEL JOHNSON, 1766.

Every woman has a right to her own silence.

ALICE MEYNELL. *Prue.*

. . . there she found inner peace, but socially she remained militant.

GEORGE SANTAYANA. *Persons and Places.*

13. WOMEN'S EDUCATION

I HAVE revisited the Lebanon.

The box-like houses which spoil its beauty have increased like Abraham's offspring, and their red tiles from Marseilles promise to last for ever. They are like measle spots on the ancient flanks of sand and limestone, a modern eruption unnecessarily ugly. But you can still escape from them and all their life by choosing a bad and stony path, which is a matter of no difficulty, and by walking a few hundred yards down any hillside. There the pagan Mediterranean world is waiting. The flat-topped pine trees cover sandy slopes with a shade which is mostly sunlight; the scent of resin is mixed with that of purple-flowering long-spiked thyme; at noonday cicadas, at sunset the frogs, sing their summer song; the sea is ever present in some triangle of grey stone at the opening of a valley; there are no houses except high up on distant shelves, and few birds and scarcely any animals in sight: and yet in these narrow solitary clefts where pools and oleanders are hidden, there is an atmosphere of ardent life, the reality of the old religion of the sun, which still endures.

Adonis and Aphrodite belong to this land, remembered by the red anemones which shelter in pits of the limestone in April, and then by the myrtle that flowers in June.

It happened that, wandering in the valley, I picked a bunch of myrtle for Mademoiselle Rose, my Syrian hostess.

She is very like Miss Matty, if you can imagine her away from Cranford, poised in this consuming land on the edge of its modern blatancy, practising a perfection of Victorian refinement for her own pleasure. She is very small, and not young, with tiny feet in pretty slippers, extremely clean and neat; she loves flowers, and Lamartine, and all the finer feelings. But when I offered my bunch of myrtle she took it coldly, and left it waterless on a chair, and finally admitted that myrtle is bad in the house, being used to plant round graves. I was sorry to see the flowers dying of neglect; on the other hand I did not like to turn my bedroom in Miss Matty's house into a mausoleum in her eyes. So I carried the little bunch down the valley again, back to its own world, and took it to a small trickling spring in whose dampness wild rhododendrons grow. I removed several derelict tins, stuck the flowers in the cool mud, and dedicated them to Aphrodite. And picking my way slowly back among the pine needles and steep stones in the breathlessness of the hot afternoon, began to wonder at the strength of these old beliefs, which still inspire thought and—on such a modest scale as mine—even action, though the gods and goddesses are exorcised or dead.

Even now, I reflected, there is more life in the tale of Adonis, known here in its own land, than there is in the teaching of most schools for girls, and as I had been talking that very morning to an education expert who was going to a feminist congress in Oxford, I fell to searching for the reasons of this comparative deadness.

Female education, when you come to consider it, is fundamentally complicated because it has to provide simultaneously for two completely different modes of life. From the beginning of Vanity, whenever that may be, till well into her middle age, a woman requires accomplishments different from—indeed, almost opposite to—those which will make her old age happy. Between these conflicting divisions of her life, her mentors have oscillated since the beginning of time. It is only in Ages of Reason (and how few and unattractive they are) that the same virtues and accomplishments will carry her right through. Even Mr. Austin, who eschewed frivolity and got his bride at twenty, referred when he proposed to her to a slightly regrettable and different past.

"If you feel secure in the unviolated integrity of your principles," he said, "be not dismayed at those slight stains upon your reputation, which a more guarded deportment, combined with my respectful and . . . *protecting* attachment, will gradually wear away."*

How few young women of any age would look forward to a "guarded deportment" as one of the attractions of matrimony. . . . The rest of his requirements were even more laborious:

"If your heart can but kindle and exalt itself into such a passion as would appease the wants of my own; if your soul is really worthy to hold communion with mine; if you can resolve to restrain the wanderings of your coquetry and your vanity—not by the purposeless or the preposterous self-denial of a Methodist—but by cultivating that quick and subtle perception of propriety, that anxious and vigilant prudence which would surround you with an atmosphere of purity and safety repulsive even to the insolence of fools; if you can determine sedulously to form yourself to that enlarged yet feminine reason, which could at once enter into my most comprehensive views and soften my technical asperities; to brace yourself up to that fortitude of affection which could wipe the damps of anguish from my forehead, or playfully teaze my sinking spirits into alacrity . . . I am convinced that I can never so utterly lose my sensibility . . . as to forget that in *me* alone is your hope and your stay. . . ."

Sarah did not appear to notice the anticlimax, accepted him, and bore his tiresomeness to the end, for she was a remarkable woman. But she had to find alleviation in Romance and German love-letters, and the fact remains that Reason and the unapparent virtues are not in themselves enough to cover the normal female span. On the other hand they must be present in some degree, or there is nothing left to a woman but to die young. She spends the first forty years of her life more or less in being looked at and in looking at herself, and measures success by her centripetal force; and for the next forty years must rely on more general pleasures and find unselfconscious amusement in the varying aspect of the world. It is the measure in which she can combine these two attitudes which constitutes her success and happiness; and hence, by the way, the belated advantage

* GORDON WATERFIELD. *Lucie Duff Gordon.*

to plain women, to whom, of course, altruism comes comparatively easy.

Teachers who, like most of us, often resemble the ostrich, rarely take into account the double requisite before them. They are either of one school or the other: dedicated—careless of outward graces—to the enlivenment of our latter end or ready, like my French friend, to say that what a woman does after forty does not matter; "she can become devotional." But there must be, one would think, some common spring to feed these two divergent rivers, some point which—comparing them to the two sides of a triangle—may include the beginnings of both. This initial point or source, somewhere embedded in the unexplored vagueness of female nature, one would like education to concentrate upon.

The ancient gods, and the quality in their tales which gives them their vitality for ever, hold an answer. For this quality lies at the root of all we can desire—every grace of art or prayer, every sincerity of speech or action; and it is the only virtue that will carry victoriously through youth and age. It is something that in our teaching we have abandoned at our peril and now hesitate to name. It is the quality of Passion; so direct, so fundamental, so naked and profound that formalists of all ages have spent the best part of their lives striving to iron it out of the souls of their pupils, denying its divine necessity and encasing it in scaffoldings of behaviour whose transience they are at no pains to make manifest. And in the measure in which they succeed, our strength declines; like Antaeus, we lose contact with our earth, and our souls die; and it is quite a miracle that women, who have been brought up on the distortion of realities ever since the invention of petticoats, should still survive as normal beings, usually in exactly the degree in which they have been able to discard the teachings of their youth.

Reticence and restraint or a more desolate emancipation— we are drilled in disembodied virtues, and rarely take the trouble to make sure that there is something to be reticent about, something to emancipate or restrain.

> They use the snaffle and the curb all right,
> But where's the bloody horse?*

* Roy Campbell.

What would we say of an electrician so anxious to avoid shocks that he tries to eliminate the current altogether? Because the spark once generated is so irresistible, because nothing in this world can withstand it, our teachers prefer to keep us far from the elemental, in sunless seclusion comforted with ornaments or bones. The same attitude has produced teetotalism, the confession of an incapacity for moderation, behind which is fear—the fear of life itself. Those things belong to the weak ages of the world, and it is a sign of returning health when many turn once more to fundamental springs, the careless Elizabethan freedom or realities of Hellas.

For there are two things to be remembered about the quality of passion.

The first is that, whatever its deep origin in life, its expression need have no particular connection with sex. It is a force which can be deviated in many directions, a sense of climax between a human being and his universe, a fearless receptivity towards the infinite Powers.

> Fire is bright,
> Let temple burn, or flax!*

The teacher's choice can lead his disciples towards the temple or the flax; but it is important that he should first see to it that the fire is there. Everything we do can be vivified by passion or remain dead without it. It is the faith that moves mountains, and also the quality that distinguishes the Psalms of David from the poems of Wilhelmina Stitch. It is passion which gives their immortality to the words of the Greek anthology, written so simply for the hopes and sorrows of ordinary men. Where it is present life cannot possibly be colourless or vain, for it discloses the vast background in whose shadow the humblest heart must move. And this is why it is a virtue to be cherished above all others in the education of women, since it confers its benefits on youth and age alike and gives dramatic value to the dullest routine.

The second point to be remembered is that the presence and not the absence of passion produces restraint. If we go through the great themes of literature and think of them

* ELIZABETH B. BROWNING. *Sonnets from the Portuguese.*

in modern journalese, we find that the root of the mischief is a devastating inability to feel. The story of Orestes, for instance:

> Father murdered in bath. Infant son waits for vengeance. Guilty mother stabbed with friend.

It is not beyond imagination.

The poet's passion alone, too deeply moved for levity, lifts the sordid chronicle into simplicity and splendour. It still exists, for the ordinary man is fortunately not as bad as the literature he inspires or the education he suffers from. He has been brought up to consider his feelings like attacks of appendicitis—pains caused by an organ now obsolete—but the forces of nature yet come to the surface. Like the sea serpent, officially unrecognized, they confront the pedant to the mutual consternation of both; and, now as ever, save man and womankind in spite of education.

14

MUTABILITY

. . . in this one thing all the discipline
Of manners and of manhood is contain'd,
A man to joyne himself with th'Universe
In his maine sway, and make (in all things fit)
One with that all, and goe on round as it:
> GEORGE CHAPMAN.   *The Revenge of Bussy D'Ambois.*

She had made herself, as it were, light, so as not to dwell
either in security or danger, but to pass between them.
> ALICE MEYNELL.   *A Woman in Grey.*

Sir, that all who are happy, are equally happy, is not true.
A peasant and a philosopher may be equally *satisfied*, but
not equally *happy*.   Happiness consists in the multiplicity
of agreeable consciousness.
> SAMUEL JOHNSON, 1766.

As if the ebbing air had but one wave.
> KEATS.   *Hyperion.*

The heavens rejoyce in motion, why should I
Abjure my so much lov'd variety.
> DONNE.   *Variety.*

Whatever mixture is in the streams, there is nothing but
pure joy in the fountain.
> RICHARD BAXTER.   *The Saints' Everlasting Rest.*

There is a certain relief in change, even though it be from
bad to worse; as I have found in travelling in a stage coach,
that it is often a comfort to shift one's position and be
bruised in a new place.
> WASHINGTON IRVING.

It is only the very wisest and the very stupidest who do
not change.
> CONFUCIUS.

Naught may endure but Mutability.
> SHELLEY.   *Mutability.*

14. MUTABILITY

IF one had to live in prison for many years, with nothing to look at but the wild, a tuft of yellow grass perhaps with the south-west wind moving through it, a clump or two of heather and the sky, such a tiny view, so restricted and yet alive, would mean more than any artist's masterpiece. Why should that be? The slightest living thing answers a deeper need than all the works of man because it is *transitory*. It has an evanescence of life, or growth, or change: it passes, as we do, from one stage to another, from darkness to darkness, into a distance where we, too, vanish out of sight. A work of art is static; and its value and its weakness lie in being so: but the tuft of grass and the clouds above it belong to our own travelling brotherhood:

> We have short time to stay as you,
> We have as short a spring;
> As quick a growth to meet decay
> As you, or anything.*

That is the bond that binds us, as Herrick saw it. That is why we love fragility, and youth, and the swiftness of the seasons: and why we go rather to an exhibition that is on for a month than to the National Gallery which is a permanent institution.

Marriage (as we are on the subject of permanent institutions) is too often a work of Art rather than Nature in this respect, a moment, so to say, frozen into permanence. Transsitoriness it lamentably lacks; and the constancy which it exacts is sometimes inertia rather than fidelity. To combine

* HERRICK. *To Daffodils.*

113

marriage with a sense of insecurity, of the delightful fragility of earthly things, is surely desirable, and should be the effort of every intelligent husband or wife. Who would not be devoted to his wife if he knew she were to be beheaded next day? Men, being on the whole more intelligent and there-fore by nature less constant than women, do frequently in-spire a sense of insecurity, and by so doing obtain a far larger percentage of adoring partners. For if it is dull always to wish to look at the same picture, eat the same dinner, wear the same clothes, why should it not be so to want always the same person beside one? And if marriage is to be the apotheosis of Habit, then surely it is a form of death. The remedy is at hand, for it is not necessary to break up a home to find variety and change; to need it so tangibly means an unimaginative self or a dull partner, and the average man or woman has enough surprises to last a married life. But the cultivation of surprise must be regarded with due honour; monotony is not to be worshipped as a virtue; nor the marriage bed treated as a coffin for security rather than a couch from which to rise refreshed.

Divine Mutability, secret of living things: it is the founda-tion of life itself. But how to introduce it into the stationary forms of art? Only by suggestion, by an appeal from what is said or painted to the inexpressible world. It is evoked by the distance left out, the word unspoken, by the broken phrases that strive dimly to reproduce something more living than themselves; by the reticence that keeps back a part and trusts to those who read or look or hear to understand.

This, it seems to me, is the test of art. The most vivid of painters is immobile: he cannot give one breath of life to equal the invisible air which bends the grass; but if he has seen it in his heart, some suggestion remains; the secret may yet be guessed at by those who know what reality lies behind his symbols and can find in his recollection as much as their own capacity supplies.

There is a charm of this kind in primitive craftsmen who, from sheer technical inability, cannot put down all they see. Their inexperience serves them well. They simplify from ignorance, as the Chinese masters simplify from knowledge. In the bay of Lindos, in the island of Rhodes, some early unrecorded navigators, weatherbound perhaps, or perhaps just resting from their labour, carved on an outstanding jag of cliff the rude form of a prow. The little detail it had is much weatherbeaten and worn away, and seems at a short distance part of the natural rock: but, through all its centuries, those few lines still hold the magic which filled the lives of the early sailors—a buoyancy of courage on their uncharted seas. No finished expert product, perfect in every detail, could fit that luminous amphitheatre of rock and sea and sun as does the rude carving religiously offered, no doubt, to some primeval god: in its few lines the imagination wanders, shackled lightly, and can fill in the changing contours of life, the passing background of islands, the wind, the flying fish and dolphins, and even the passage of time—all that the artist knew and could not tell.

In literature it is the same. W. P. Ker used to say that the charm of old ballads lies in the fact that, repeated by word of mouth from generation to generation, the non-essential has gradually dropped and been lost; the naked structure remains, to be clothed every time afresh by the imagination of the reader. We do not deal, when we write, only with words we use: we deal also with all those which, unspoken, come to the reader's mind: it is not what we actually *say*, it is what we make *him* think and see that counts as literature; and our words are a mere surface, beyond which should lie the living universe, or as much of it as all our powers can span.

This strength of evocation gives to all art such life as it has and, by eliminating rigid outlines, brings it as near as may be to life itself. But it is not only in art or marriage that the immutable, the want of elasticity, is eventually synonymous with death. It is just as much so in the world of ideas, of politics, institutions and religions. Constancy, far from being a virtue, seems often to be the besetting sin of the human race, daughter of laziness and self-sufficiency, sister of sleep, the cause of most wars and practically all persecutions. We are for ever crystallizing, attempting to imprison what is fluid into a permanent form. Religions are the most obvious examples—dams designed for eternity against the innate momentum of the human race. Their failure to petrify the natural inconstancy of man is made conspicuous by the greatness of the things with which they deal, but the story of any code or committee points the same moral, and in his *History of Civilization* Buckle makes an illuminating remark when he says that almost every reform consists in the clearing away of an old rather than in the making of a new law.

In this country we have hitherto had one great merit in the eyes of history: we have done our best to recognize the laws of change.

The British are rigid only in trifles—matters of dress or manners at table : their constitution, their laws, their religion, their policies and many of their principles are formless and vague, based on foundations so accidental as to be almost grotesque. They are a perpetual problem to rational neighbours, who do not recognize in this formlessness, vagueness, and imperceptible capacity for transition the law of life itself. They embody an effort, however blind, to work *with* rather than *against* the cosmic mutability of things.

With us no sudden jerk, or only a very small one, is necessary to slip from one idea or revolution to another. We do not put our codes or constitutions down in writing; when we do so—as with the Thirty-Nine Articles—we refer to them with embarrassment and think of them as rarely as we can. For we do know dimly that the imprisoned word is death, and that the human vice of Constancy is but an expression of man's irrepressible tendency to consider his own ideas alone as final in a universe that moves.

15

LOVE

Dye your wool once purple and what water will cleanse it
of that stain?

ST. JEROME.

And love her towers of dread foundation laid
Under the grave of things;

WORDSWORTH.   Sonnet.

. . . the nightingales in the thicket of ilex should sing to
me like my own heart.

GEORGE SANTAYANA.   *Dialogues in Limbo.*

. . . by love alone
God binds us to Himself and to the hearth,
And shuts us from the waste beyond His peace.

W. YEATS.   *The Land of Heart's Desire.*

And ought not to be prophan'd on either part,
For though 'tis got by *chance*, 'tis kept by *art*.

DONNE.   *The Expostulation.*

But . . . the truth as I imagine is that whether such
practices are honourable or . . . dishonourable is not a
simple question; they are honourable to him who follows
them honourably, dishonourable to him who follows them
dishonourably. . . .   Evil is the vulgar lover who loves the
body rather than the soul, inasmuch as he is not even stable,
because he loves a thing which is in itself unstable . . .
whereas the love of the noble disposition is life-long,

PLATO.   *Symposium.*

The lyf so short, the craft so longe to lerne,
Th'assay so sharp, so hard the conquerynge,
The dredful joye alwey that slit so yerne,
Al this mene I be Love. . . .

CHAUCER.   *The Parlement of Foules.*

15. LOVE

THE women of Cyprus are, on the whole, rather plain. They walk up and down among their steep vineyards in the sun, labouring with kilted skirts, and laced boots to keep their ankles firm on the rough paths, and weights of hay or faggots on their backs. When a stranger rose among them from the sea, she had no need to be superlatively lovely: and one goes with some misgiving westward to Paphos, wondering whether Aphrodite was not perhaps overpraised in her day? New Paphos itself is a dull and orphaned shore, more reminiscent of the landing of St. Paul, and of the toil and disappointments of life, than of the Mother of Gods and men. Aphrodite, however, did not land exactly there but at a place a little farther to the east, called White Rocks, where the remains of a temple are on a head-land, above a bay of polished boulders and white sand.

Here the long waves still lift their backs as if they carried the queen of the world, and come in ranks with a space between them, regiments saluting, with the morning shining through the pennants and the plumes, the tossing spray. The water has the gem-like lucidity of the Levant and shows every pebble clean-cut through the advancing wave. There are no trees about, but the swelling shapes of grassy hills heavy with spicy odours in the sun; and a simplicity, an absence of clefts or crannies, an open-ness not cooled by shadows, but by the movement of the air and water, the bare world rolling. Here someone, a shepherd or a seaman, saw Loveliness, and gave to the surrounding rocks for ever, to the sapphire horizon and the whispering foam, the secret which the human being is happy to know, perhaps only

LOVE

once—when he sees the eyes of his beloved deeper than ocean
and the Goddess herself in their radiance, miraculous and
alas! unembraceable as the whiteness that bore her.

No creature can ever be derelict who has had this moment.
He is an initiate. He has seen the well of life rising suddenly
within its fleshly walls; out of the dark unknown foundations
of the world, emerging from chaos, the glowing stream has
risen stronger, more ancient, more divine, than the sweet
human form that contains it; and the current has met above
his being and carried him along its dark perennial way.

Love, and the beloved, are different. The lightness, the
grace, the breath of divinity, are no intrinsic part of the
shape which they inhabit. They radiate from it and lie like
enchantment on all the world around. He is not completely happy who cannot remember this fugitive visit, this
murmur of doves about him in his spring; when the skies
are doors just opening and the grass lies like gold upon the
hills; and the cries in the street are music, and the old men
smile as they pass and remember their days.

The Goddess soon or late gathers the hem of sea and sky
about her and departs; the colours fade; the White Rocks
remain bare in the sun; the magic is over. The veil of
divinity no longer hides the form of the beloved, and all is
common day.

Then comes love as we chiefly know it in our lives, and
as Botticelli painted his later Venus, with sad young eyes too
innocent, that look out shrinkingly on toil and sorrow. The
sea still ridges her shell with little flecks of foam; the winds
still wrap their gentle mantles round her; yet she is conscious
of nakedness, no longer triumphant, and weak in a fearful
world. This is the love that walks in our lives and shares
their toil and stumbles; and clothes itself, if it is wise, in the
memory of that other time when all things were divine.

The whole human endeavour is to keep intact at least the
outward adornments of that first visitation: like the riderless
horse, or the empty armour, they are borne through the slow
funeral procession of the life that follows Love when it departs.

Where men and women are wise and fortunate they have
allowed no break between the vision and its memory, so that
these merge imperceptibly, and no one, least of all themselves,

120

can tell when the light that was unearthly turned into day. But even where this is not so, and death or division or the rashness of the heart or the grinding of need have stained the memory and spoiled it—the colours that remain, however few and however eaten into and effaced almost by time, still keep the divine quality that first made them alive. This divinity often leaves the form it once made beautiful; it shines on other loves, or illuminates even the unexpected details and trivial daily things that one would think incapable of answering to that glow. So, on a low flat coast, the presence of the sea is felt far inland and out of sight of the sea: salt is on the lips, and the salt-loving tamarisk blossoms in the ditches, and lavender or thrift cling to chalky ledges: the colour-wash on houses is bleached and bitten on one side by the prevailing wind; the rivers slow down as they meet sandbanks, and there is a gleam of sea-shells on the gravel of paths that tend to sand: in the softness and the freshness of the air, in the clouds wreathed in high spirals from their flat watery base, the lover who once has known it recognizes the nearness of the sea. And perhaps in a gap between dull houses and fences of allotments, and labelled pleasures, he may get a glimpse of that deeper blue horizon where he once saw the free Aphrodite born of foam.

Everything therefore depends on the visitation of the Gods and, as this is unpredictable, separate human arrangements have had to be made. It is no fault of theirs, and yet a thing to be remembered, that at every moment their pattern must cut across the divine.

For this reason every sort of social code is unsatisfactory, and the chances of happiness in love appear to be more or less equal under any dispensation that gives to the human creature a reasonable degree of freedom. Tacitly, under most systems, an allowance is made for the interruption of the Gods.

In Latin countries it is expected on the whole to come after, in the northern ones before marriage: in the Muslim East it is hampered altogether and only now beginning to uncoil itself from the too inelastic supremacy of man (though it was in the East that the words of forgiveness were spoken to the woman who "loved much"). The Latin way has a great deal to recommend it; it concentrates on the accessories, on teaching, as it were, the mechanism of love, so that the years may run smoothly in their grooves and, if the vision comes, may find ground tilled and weeded and ready to bear easily whatever the seed may be. If fortune favours and the parents' judgment was careful, and the young themselves were free and candid in their amount of choice, love follows marriage as faithfully and deeply as it does in more independent lands: otherwise it will come as a stranger, and fit itself with more or less disturbance—but on the whole rather less—into the normal rut of things. The easy habitual sex life makes for indulgence, but it prevents the miseries of repression, the solitary twists that happen too often with northern natures: and I think that men and women live more easily together in the south.

Yet we in the north have dreams. We may wait fruitless years on an arid shore, but when love comes we hope to see the Goddess herself. Like all devotees, we risk our temporal chances for hopes that have a measure of eternity. And though many fail altogether, and most fail in part—their enduring moment has been. It is a bond between them, too, for all that it is often a bond of failure, and is strong in human ways; for many lives, unconsciously, in their dull habitual reaches, still remember that forgotten glow of dawn. Perhaps the *only* reason for preferring our northern system to the more practical methods of the south is the isolation, as it were, of this moment: it is not crowded out and made unimportant by habits of more easy intercourse: it is put into an open space of our youth, cleared and empty, where—if it has come at all—it may be seen for ever down the vista of years. In respect of this moment alone it becomes a sin for human beings to unite, whether in marriage or without it, except in love. And what happens after matters very little, and will indeed be richer by the riches of that time.

I have figured this division of north and south, but it is independent of latitude, and is one of those unbridgeable clefts of the human race, such as the division between women who wear real lace or none upon their underwear, and those who, like the lady in Meredith, "prefer twenty shillings to one sovereign." As in the contrast of religions, it is not a

difference of good and bad, but it is important to live in the
category to which one naturally belongs.

Each has its own danger. The moment may be waited for,
and because of the very ignorance produced by the waiting
may pass unrecognized when it comes; or else it may come
when a life too full of unimportant things has blunted the
power to receive it and accidents, or the callousness of others,
are there to interfere. No crime short of murder can be
comparable to the crime of destroying in another the capacity
to love: and this happens sometimes through the rashness of
parents, or the sight of misery in adolescence, but more often
through some bitterness of experience when youth is still
defenceless, "nullo contusus aratro," and wounds leave a
scar difficult to heal.

But when all is said and done the choice lies in ourselves.
We are suitors to love, and life is more generous than Bas-
sanio's father-in-law: the caskets it presents are just as enig-
matic, the choice as difficult and full of doom, but the result
is not usually quite so final, and the Prince of Morocco was
no doubt able to open another box in his time.

Safety lies in awareness of love: not in this person nor in
that, by some private shore or secret enclosed harbour, but
in the consciousness of all as a part of its embracing sea.
All continents and islands, not our shore alone, are surrounded by the network of those streams; the tides that fill
the creeks are swung by the whole globe in commerce with
its stars, and by their planetary motion the smallest clinging
shell-fish of the rocks is fed; nor is there any division between
the shallower girdle of the coasts and those depths where
hurricanes and blind monsters as well as the friendly dews and
rains of earth are born. Embraced by this infinitude, we
step for our summer pleasure into the wayward foam; and
think of love in the same way, when it fills our pools and roams
with its light and echo in our caves. Its tides come from
distances far greater than the coastline they embrace can
dream; and when they recede we can but keep our faith
and feed our eyes with a horizon enriched with what lies
beyond it, and rest in the certainty that at any moment,
in youth or age or sorrow, in small ways or great, the divine
Aphrodite may return with the splendour of the world

iridescent and fragile as foam in her arms. The waves will laugh and cover the bare rocks and worn shabby places of our hearts; and we shall know how to welcome her, because we have known her long ago.

16

SORROW

The same incarnat traitor routeth in all hearts;
> BRIDGES. *Testament of Beauty*, IV, 749.

.... and many, passing the same course before us, framed
for us weary paths, through which we were fain to pass.
> ST. AUGUSTINE. *Confessions.*

With the strange cry of swans the pools are shrill:
The nightingale beneath the poplar shade
Singeth, as though remembering the passion,
Forgetful of the pain.
She sings, I hold my peace:
For when will come my spring?

11th century.   Trans. by Helen Waddell in *The Wandering Scholars.*

e nella tua memoria i dî felici,
e il tuo dolore dentro le tue mani
come un'urna che reggi . . .
> GABRIELE D'ANNUNZIO.   *Fedra.*

. . . the vast shadow of the temple still stood between him
and the sun.
> GEORGE SANTAYANA.   *Character and Opinion in the U.S.A.*

It does not matter what the whip is; it is none the less a
whip, because you have cut thongs for it out of your own
souls.
> JOHN RUSKIN.   *Crown of Wild Olive.*   On War.

. . . the man is yet to come
Who hath not journeyed in this native hell.
> KEATS.   *Endymion*, IV.

16. SORROW

THE long history of man has not yet reconciled him to sorrow. Pain and fear and hunger are effects of causes which can be foreseen and known: but sorrow is a debt which someone else makes for us, or we pile it up in ignorance, unaware of the items that are to be exacted when the day for payment comes; and therefore man rebels, unavailingly but unsubdued, down all the cycles of his generations.

Long before words were written or perhaps even spoken, one among our forebears revolted in his heart against the injustice of fate and so became different from his surroundings, and the founder of civilization: for this was the beginning of law, of rigour and mercy, of all the human order; it was the beginning of something which in their freedom even the Gods cannot know.

> O Thou who didst with pitfall and with gin
> Beset the path I was to wander in,
> Thou wilt not with predestination round
> Enmesh me, and impute my fall to sin.*

Not quite, but almost, for the dice seem loaded. And the warmth we feel at the sight of one man or a few fighting against numbers, Thermopylae, or Dunkirk, or the solitary breach defended, is perhaps an echo of the belief that in our own soul every one of us is up against the odds of all the world.

> Denn ich bin ein Mensch gewesen,
> Und dass heisst ein Kämpfer sein.†

* E. FITZGERALD. *Omar Khayyam.*
† GOETHE. *The Poet and the Houri.*

We know there is danger round the corner for even the
happiest. It is this that makes the innocence of childhood
stab so sharply, in which—if you come to think of it—there is
no intrinsic merit; but we see it as it cannot see itself—walking into destruction—and if childhood is abused it brings our
human patience to an end. It is as if the only truce were
betrayed, the one sanctuary broken, and fate revealed there
with her bloody hands, treading unlawful ground.

Such was the sight of Naples when I landed there in 1945,
after six years of war. The carelessness which the city used
to wear so gaily in its poverty had vanished; dull people,
and few, walked in the streets. I watched them, and saw
none stop and speak to another: the prosperous houses were
shuttered, and the shops below them unfurnished. A small
commerce of misery was carried on half-heartedly by pedlars
of worthless wares round paltry booths; even vice, ubiquitous
and intangible, could scarcely be called by that name—there
was no virtue with which to compare it. And the children
roamed untended. They played no game, but begged or
shuffled in the squalor of the gutters, or stole, and sat in door-
ways with pinched masks of faces, or slept there with heads
pillowed on their arms. They all seemed dumb. And I
fled from the streets and shut myself up in the bedroom of my
hotel, where the sordid ruins of war—cracked mirror and
makeshift towels and broken lampshade—at least were not
alive.

In the corner of history, as in those seventeenth century
maps decorated with mythological engravings, one might
place the figure of Sorrow building her slow heap—building
it with all things visible and invisible, the columns of temples
and fragments of custom corrupted with private cruelty:

"Ces murs redoubtables s'élèvent sur le fondement des
mensonges antiques, par l'art subtil et féroce des légistes,
des magistrats et des princes."*

It would be well for us if sorrow came from magistrates
and princes only. It is more deeply rooted. It stands in
our landscape like the pyramids in Egypt whose shapes seem
alien when first you see them with lengthening shadows across

* ANATOLE FRANCE. *Opinions de Jérôme Coignard.*

the fertile cultivation and burnished aisles of palms. The peasant walks in his slim thin gown along the dyke, with bare flat feet, and his buffaloes before him, and the shadows of these tyrants' monuments lie slanting across his way. There is no escape from them in the narrow way of civilization. And they have been seen so long across the panoramas of history, and have been gilded by so many sunsets that they come to be scarcely noticed, their human superfluous origin forgotten—the long agony of the building and lash of the contractor's whip; they are part of the surrounding desert and their sharp segments are never out of sight. And they are not unfriendly when they are looked at from flat roofs across the cotton fields in flower, in that hour when the smoke curls up from under the cooking pot and children's voices lift in the air like bells, and the white ibis fly to their evening branches across the embers of the sky: there would be a blank and a strangeness if in the background of peaceful living the shapes of sorrow were nowhere to be seen.

During the war, towards the end of 1940, I happened to be in Cairo, persuading young Egyptians—in that year of disaster—that Hitler and Mussolini were to fail in spite of all. It was good work, with friends in it and new experience, but it meant about fourteen hours of argument for every day except Sundays, and a time came when an interval of silence seemed essential, and two of us found a woman who kept tents on the desert ridge behind the pyramids, with beds and food and water, and we drove out and left the car with a canvas cover over it in the sand, and for a whole week forgot the allurements of democracy and the strategy of the war and looked across to the opposite desert ridge and watched the valley of the Nile that lay between, an easy span but rich under harvests, dense with villages and straight water-ways, where the mists lay low even when the outer stars were clear at night, and the dim half-lights of Cairo—whose street lamps were painted blue for air-raids—shone with a gentle phosphorescence embowered in trees.

Then, close beside us, the pyramids appeared in their desert shape. Their smooth pink stones visited only by the revolving light and its changing hours, with the patina of centuries upon them, curved like the roundness of earth under the sun or stars. The worn and broken tiers had lost the feel of man's hand; one could not think of a human agency in their building; nor, as one rode west or south over ribs and wind-scattered plains of gravel, could one imagine a free horizon clear of those triangular forms.

We used to walk behind or around them on our way to Mena, and noticed in the colossal shadows of their base how all around is death—a vast congregation of tombs not peacefully bedded like ours at home, that turn again to life—but honeycombed elaborately, planned to endure, watched over through years and years, centuries and centuries, by the living who excavated and decorated them under the desert soil. No other human monuments stand like the pyramids in the rank of a work of nature, yet they are but mausoleums built by man to bury his own kind. As I walked every day to fetch the post between the great base and the shrivelled acres of the rifled tombs, I would look at my hand—so strangely and cosily alive in the warm sun—and rest it against the tiers of stone and think of the grief that had made them: until Sorrow itself seemed a pyramid, built course upon course as a legacy from man to man in times so bitter and remote that its human origins are now forgotten, though it weighs on our horizon and darkens it with loneliness.

Sorrow separates us from our fellowship. Loneliness pads like a eunuch behind it and draws the black seraglio curtains and shuts it into privacy, in a sanctuary where the heart and mind are segregated from the world to which they belong. Let these curtains but open and the greater part of sorrow would vanish in the unity of all created things.

What chaos would reign in a human body whose every cell acted for itself, or only for the few neighbouring cells with blood or tissue similar to its own! Even a hurt finger makes the pulse flutter and the nerves retract, and the absence of such response means mortification or disease: yet the same phenomenon, a cold deadness to pain not in China or the Antipodes but in the house next door, in the people we meet and speak with every day, in our loves and friends and parents —symptoms which in a human body ask for medical attention—are taken in the body of this world to be part of a divine Order and immutable Law.

The cure of most grief could be found in unity, a cosmic integrity and sympathy of all. The saints and sages who try to practise it in their solitary cells have as yet to base their happiness outside a world where the separateness, the disease of earth, is strong. Yet it is a comfort even in our sickness to know that health exists, and to believe that our suffering is no necessary strand of destiny, no heartless torment where the heart of things should be, but a disorder, a deadness of sensibility, a want of function in what is meant to be a whole. The scientist looks hopefully towards the landscape that still lies before him unexplored; and so may men look upon the yet untravelled roads of love that lie before them, and see the ending of sorrow at their end.

> Some say, the lark makes sweet division;
> This doth not so, for she divideth us:*

The division of music has been turned to discord. But it is by human voices only. And even so and now, in the waste where the sons of Cain must wander, some note of fellowship and pity will often ring out and warm the heart, and lead it with a swift response to reaffirm the bond that lies hidden under our sad evasions, to make a blessing out of the curse of grief.

Envy is chief minister of our loneliness and cause of almost all our sorrow. Through him we forget that the joys of others are tributaries of our stream; we build a solitary barrier to guard some poor trickle of our own—too meagre for hearts that need the universe to beat with, the happiness of all to feed them, the pain of all to share. Yet even in our partial awareness and imperfect love, the grief that shadows others has often more power to restrain us than any threatening of ourselves; and opens as it were a window on to a world where all griefs must be felt by all as their own, and little of sorrow need be suffered except mortality, which can be peacefully accepted among our natural steps in time.

Many years have gone by since such unhappiness met me as leaves one stranded on the floor of the world, never to fear hurt or fall again. There is a story of Kipling's about a man who remembered himself as a Roman galley slave, in the last fight in which he drowned; when the rowers,

Romeo and Juliet.

chained to their benches, saw the thin water-line above the sinking bulwark—their last vision of the daylight and the sun. Even so I had to wait at that time, chained as it were, and knew that grief was coming, and knew what it would be; and nothing in life or time could avert it. I was then in Bologna, in a hotel that looked out on houses, whose lower roofs of warm red tiles are still in my sight to-day, though probably demolished long ago.

It was June, and some young women were sitting at the open windows, or moving about far back in their room where they were invisible to the street but open to me from above: and so, even through the deadness of my sorrow, I began to notice that there was something unfamiliar to me about them, a taste "of poisonous brass and metals sick," as they strolled naked inside their room, or threw a mere piece of stuff about them when they came to the window. They were cheerful and unconcerned, exchanging repartee with young men in the street, and—I could not help remarking—singularly sluttish and unattractive to look at. It seems strange to tell now, but I had no idea at that time—being very young and gently brought up—that such a thing as a brothel existed; but I looked at them vaguely with a gradually dawning feeling of distaste.

The afternoon was wearing towards evening, and, as I waited there, the swallows came out. They flew above the small tiled roofs that cover each chimney pot, and high into the sky above the line of Apennine beyond: in their aerial tumult, with needle wings, they embroidered a network constantly vanishing, constantly renewed, behind which the sunset unfolded its roll of gold. The late hour rested like a hand on the roofs of the town, and into my grief a certainty of inviolable peace came fleeting and eternal. The news that I had waited for reached me, and broke upon me as the wave broke on the men chained to their oars—as it breaks upon us all: days and weeks and months followed, lost in forgetfulness; but the memory of that afternoon survived with its strange peace. In it all was unified, painted as it were in a picture—the darting swallows and the young men in the street and the brothel windows and my own passion, reconciled with each other in a sheaf of earthly light long pardoned by time.

17

CHOICE AND TOLERATION

But the stately ruins thereof give a shadow of its beauty while it flourished in its pride.

CHAPLAIN TO THE MISSION FROM QUEEN ELIZABETH TO JEHANGIR, *describing Chitor.*

And everything but stone had passed away
That made them lovely in that vanished day.

WILLIAM MORRIS. *The Earthly Paradise.*

The vast heap of human frailty.

SANNAZARO. Sonnet.

Set the foot down with distrust upon the crust of the world
—it is thin.

EDNA ST. VINCENT MILLAY. *Underground System.*

La clémence du temps est plus sûre que celle des hommes.

ANATOLE FRANCE. *Opinions de Jérôme Coignard.*

White shall not neutralize the black, nor good
Compensate bad in man, absolve him so;
Life's business being just the terrible choice.

BROWNING. *The Ring and the Book.*

For man can adde weight to heavens heaviest curse.

DONNE. *To Sir Edward Herbert at Julyers.*

... the boom of the surges of Chaos on the dykes of the world.

W. P. KER. *The Dark Ages.*

17. CHOICE AND TOLERATION

THE man who weeds is usually looked upon as innocent, mild and harmless, an avoider of complexity, a lover of peace, to whom the gentleness of nature opens when the soil is moist and yielding and neither powdered with drought nor sodden with rain. On such days, when the sun finds woolly leaves that hold dew in shady corners, the travelling bees and thin flies with straightlaced figures, and beetles with hard metal business wings, and butterflies uncertain of their way come wandering through the garden, each with an idea of his own as to what the defect may be that divides the weeds and flowers. The true gardener then brushes over the ground with slow and gentle hand, to liberate a space for breath round some favourite; but he is not thinking about destruction except incidentally. It is only the amateur like myself who becomes obsessed and rejoices with a sadistic pleasure in weeds that are big and bad enough to pull, and at last, almost forgetting the flowers altogether, turns into a Reformer.

Reformers are tiresome people, but what is one to do? Tolerance, too, makes the home unfit to live in. My god-father used to say that an Englishman considers himself broadminded only when he is upholding convictions the opposite of his own. I remember one such during the war. He was a colonel commanding a camp for Italian internees in whom I was interested: our friends among the prisoners were browbeaten by the Fascists, flogged when they read the newspaper provided by us at great expense, and forced to sing the Mussolini hymn at meal-times: the Colonel left them to it, refusing to interfere, on the ground that "Fascists, too, must be allowed to be patriotic."

CHOICE AND TOLERATION

The most disastrous scene of tolerance I have witnessed was not an affair of human beings at all, but a drama of the mineral and vegetable worlds, a war between trees and ruins in the deserted city of Mandu. Here, in central India, on a wooded ridge like a moraine that overhangs the endless plain, one of those small and swift Muhammedan dynasties of Mogul times sprang up and died: and before it did so, built stone memorials of its gaiety and beauty that still survive, lovely and derelict islands, among the glades of the jungle.

We drove up here one day, when the hot weather had already begun and the rain bird had uttered its yelling brainless cry; when the leaves of trees drooped through noon over the fainting fields. In the Arab summer there is, as it were, a mineral endurance: strength withdraws itself into the veins of the rocks and secret chasms of water, and leaves no vulnerable surface open to the sun. But in these park-lands of central India the strong soil wrestles with the heat and holds it in its arms and drinks it in, and lies vanquished as in a lassitude of love, transfused, and alive in its stillness. And the dawn, transparent as a sea-shell washed up on the wet sand, finds no quick response—as it does in Arabia, flushing upon the brows of naked cliffs—but spreads its pageant remote in the wide sky, above the quiet unresponsive trees. The grey monkeys wake and slide from wayside branches into the warming dust, and flocks of green parrots fly to forage in the fields. Here, as the light strengthens, the sun cuts its way with sudden crescents and bright scimitars into the well-spaced avenues that line the Indian roads; and swiftly, as into an open sea, we push out to the fullness of the day.

A Hindu village had lingered on beside the deserted halls of Mandu, and was celebrating its annual fair. Carts filled with bright *saris* and women's gay talkative faces and a tumult of anklets and bangles and heavy black coiled hair, creaked and swayed up the ridge, drawn by dust-coloured oxen, nonchalant and slow, on whose backs lay the branching shadows of the jungle. Towards walls hidden and overgrown and a crumbling gate that pierced them, thin-legged country-men were climbing by a stone-flagged way. To them Mandu is but a village of the numberless villages that appear mono-tonous in central India as stationary waves upon a sea.

Beside its palace walls they unharnessed their cattle and
tilted their booths and stretched their crazy awnings against
the sun, and laid out the various grains and nuts of their
fields and spicy cooked things wrapped in leaves, and coloured pedlars' wares. They bathed in the tank whose
springs no doubt decided the choice of this height for the
building of the city in its day. The women's secluded
harems in the palaces are now ruined and forgotten: men and
women splashed in the same water, cool and green in the
shadow of the masonry; the wet *saris* clung to slim bodies,
dusky as ripe grapes; the young girls wrung out their smoothly-
parted hair and coiled it up again, and slipped the new dress
for the feast out of its cotton wrapping and donned it at the
water's edge. They played there, gay and vivid as dragon-
flies in the shortness of their day; and when the sun began to
etch the branches of the trees, the carts were loaded and
departed down the slanting road that cuts the jungle.

Then the modern life shrank back into its hovels and small
fields, and rested in apparent peace under the evening light,
while around it a siege continued uninterrupted and un-
observed—the slow eating of the ruins by the trees.

They have already swallowed the undistinguished quarters
of the city; their glades have covered the traces of streets
and squares. The mosque stands, with smooth walls, and
aisles on rough-hewn piers, one of the noblest mosques in
India: and so do the royal tombs built square on platforms.
The shorn water palace dreams between its artificial sheets
of water, whose stone edges the forest has broken down. Here
flying steps, unbanistered, soar up to terraces and jutting
windows and pagodas—volatile thoughts chiselled and made
safe, as they hoped, in stone. All this is preserved and stands,
though, even here, the forest roots have buckled the courtyard
paving stones, and it is but a truce. The city must once have
been extended widely on its height: its walls on the jungle
slopes are made visible by the high crowns of the trees they
feed. And the tombs of its forgotten inhabitants, square and
dome-surmounted Mogul tombs, are spread a great way
down the road as one descends.

Many have already sunk into heaps, sucked shapeless by
the roots in which they are entwined; some, fissured and

lop-sided, carry whole trees fattened and relentless into the
sunlight. The random seeds that were harboured and throve
on the lime of the masonry, and pushed their threadlike fingers
unresisted into cracks of stone or rubble, have now become
monsters with swollen necks that feed on these defeated
pieties of men; and the unrecognizable mounds, the cracked
and blistered plaster, the fragments of ornament and marble
show every step in the long stairway whose beginning is
tolerance and whose end is decay.

Tolerance cannot afford to have anything to do with the
fallacy that evil may convert itself to good.

In the dark central crisis of his life Shakespeare came to
realize that goodness cannot *convert*. This is the secret, I
believe, of his greatest plays. In *King Lear*, the Duke of
Albany declares to Goneril that "wisdom and goodness to the
vile seem vile." The New Testament does likewise. The
seed that falls on stony ground must die, and there is never a
hope for the goats (though it seems a pity that sheep are chosen
as emblems of the virtuous). To call upon sinners is different;
they are mixed, and the best in us answers: for goodness is
loved at sight. If evil could *see*, it would cease. But evil
is by its nature incapable of sight, and unable to understand
what goodness is; and the whole art of corruption therefore
begins by training the victims to be *incapable of comprehending
good*. "The heart's division divideth. . . ." The simply
virtuous are unaware of division, and their unawareness—a
state of rubble and plaster like the tombs of Mandu—is the
stuff of tragedy: it causes an exasperation, an encouragement,
an excitement of evil.

This happens over and over again in Shakespeare's
tragedies. The goodness, the generosity, the innocence of
Prospero, Cordelia, Troilus, Duncan, Desdemona, are the
door by which all horror enters. In *King Lear*, a justification
is given to Nemesis by the old man's foibles: it is carefully
contradicted by the character of Gloucester, who has no other
reason for prominence in the play, who suffers equally with
his king, and for such slight offence. In *Timon of Athens* the
problem is crudely shown and our sense of proportion revolts,
perhaps because even now we are not as inured to injustice
as was the Tudor world: but the play is one of the most

interesting because, so nakedly presented, it has probably preserved the first form in which it held the poet's thoughts. The theme, often repeated, must have been strongly present in the author's mind.

Where the idea of conversion does not exist, virtue is regarded as a state of detachment. It is strong as a tower is strong, in a defensive way, secure on its foundations, but static, and not mobile for attack. It triumphs at last, because it is unassailable in itself, a shelter and a bulwark for its adherents. It minds its own business, and toleration, in the sense only of non-interference, follows as a matter of course.

Conversion is recognised to be impossible in advertisement or war, where mistakes are either visible or deadly: no business firm or commanding general would think to succeed by concentrating on the shoddiness of others rather than on the excellence of his own. But in preaching and in propaganda, we still think to convert, and this fallacy makes us either wholeheartedly interfering or modestly ashamed, and anyway robs us of warmth and passion, making a dowdiness of our idea of good.

The true secret of persuasiveness is that it *never* converts: it speaks to its own only, and discovers to them the unexpected secrets of their hearts.

For seven years, during the war and after, I was engaged in one way or another on the art of persuasion, which I would call propaganda if that unfortunate word were not doomed to swing with opposite meanings between Herr Goebbels and St. Paul. In all that time we never troubled about what our adversaries said, but stuck to our own story, which was good enough.

Our Ministry, we hoped, felt apostolic too, but was surprisingly apologetic towards its own gospels, and reluctant to prod the lions in its path with anything sharp enough for a lion to mind. There was an assumption that efficient propaganda is indecent; only bungling could make it excusable.

How different is this from the gift of tongues—how timid and how base. The right way if we have something to say is to say it plainly—not for conversion, but for such as may be waiting for our voice.

From their high Olympus, as the last of their gifts, the Gods gave free-will to man, and with it laid upon him the burden of choice, and made everything in all his worlds depend on the choice that he made. Out of the humility of his choice is his tolerance born: for he sees his brothers taking paths different from his own, and finds it hard to think himself better than they: until in his perplexity he comes to surmise that there may be freedom only, and never a choice at all. This is the very wilderness of toleration.

Let him choose for himself with such care that he may not fear to give his reasons, but be ready, like some honest country-man, to point out a direction to those who wish to travel in the region that he knows: and then he will find himself in a company larger than he had ever thought, of such as like the roughness and adventure of his way. And let this be his tolerance, that he knows those who travel by other paths to be out of hearing, and that the variety of choice was infinite at the start: therefore he will not trouble them to join him, but out of his confidence in his own way will cast his eye over the open landscape and watch their progress, with a detached and friendly and interested mind: and not call it tolerance to be afraid of his own choice, or afraid to give the reasons of its making, but let his humility lie rather in remembering how hard in its time it was to make. And if he is inclined to missionary undertakings, let him remember that his knowledge of the country is useful only to those who wish to travel in his path.

18

TRAVEL

When life runs low and ways are dark, my scholar is the booking-clerk . . .

Sir W. Raleigh's Letters.

It pleases me to see the Earth in the Crowds of the Planets.

DE FONTENELLE. *A Plurality of Worlds.*

. . . the world that lay
Before me in my endless way.

WORDSWORTH. *Stepping Westward.*

For peregrination charms our senses with such unspeakable and sweet variety, that some count him unhappy that never travelled, a kind of prisoner, and pity his case that from his cradle to his old age beholds the same still; still, still the same, the same:

BURTON. *Anatomy of Melancholy.*

Iam mens praetrepidans avet vagari;
Iam laeti studio pedes vigescunt.
O dulces comitum valete coetus,
Longe quos simul a domo profectos,
Diversae variae viae reportant.

CATULLUS. *Iturus in Asiam.*

Where could you ever be a stranger,
Bearing your own delight and danger
And always young?

DOUGLAS LE PAN. *Rider on the Sands.*

. . . our ships are now content to sail
About these happy islands that we know.

WILLIAM MORRIS. *The Earthly Paradise.*

And God hath spread the earth as a carpet for you, that ye may walk therein through spacious paths.

Quran, LXXI.

18. TRAVEL

ONE charm about our town is that there is nothing here
to do. I mean by this that there is no "season," no
formal entertaining, no bridge, no sport, no golf. The
bank manager has what he calls a retriever and goes out now
and then on a Sunday, dressed in brown velvet, with a gun;
and now and then one meets a peasant, bent like the man in
the moon, with a faggot of twigs limed with mistletoe under one
arm, and on his other wrist an owl tied by a string by which
he lures smaller birds to their fate. There are two cinemas,
one run by the Municipality and the other expurgated by the
Church, and a theatre built recently in the castle of the
Queen of Cyprus, where an Eleonora Duse commemoration
or a travelling play, or even a dance, is offered now and then.
With a car one can reach the Dolomites or the Lido, but these
are games outside the city orbit. The only regular entertain-
ments that actually belong to us are the arrivals and departures
of the motor buses to Padova and Treviso, which we may
witness every day in comfort from under the yellow awnings
of the café in the square, over a vermouth and bitters.

This happy emptiness on the horizon of our entertainment
enhances the leisure for walking, which is delightful anyway
among our hills, so small, so gay and diverse in outline, so
gently spread to the sun with their patches of fruit-trees and
harvests. Every time of year is good among them except
when high summer draws storms towards the northern
mountains and our foothills, like the lesser people of this
world, catch the worst of the downpour when it falls. Even
in January there are Christmas roses in small and rocky dells
tumbling through brushwood; and in February, when the

year begins, a sky of snowdrops appears round every stream. When the grass is still bleached like tow, the broken ground opens to flowers—hepaticas, blue and white violets, periwinkles; then primroses, and the dog-tooth violet with glaucous leaves, and bugloss and green hellebore: all these come with the mouse-ear leaflets of the budding hazel copses, before the April puffs of blossom, pink and then white, break everywhere like smoke. In the depth of later spring, when the apple trees have ceased to flower, the interest shifts to the plain: corn in rectangular fields is ripening like a quilt of bronze and green; and every hailstorm and thundercloud is watched with fear. The peasants used to be able to pay insurance against hail, but that too has lapsed with the war, and now their only help is the church bell's tolling, a dark warning sound when the heavy clouds bear down.

The autumn harvests are maize in the plain, and vines on the easy slopes, and chestnuts and apples on the hillsides; and the country glows under them like a Bronze Age shield, with the story of its trees and tillage and poplar-outlined roads and S-shaped streams beaten on it in copper and gold.

Autumn and winter are best for walking. There is a bite in the air that lifts the feet easily, under the wayward last warmth of the sun. When that, too, goes, and the rims of dead leaves lie rigid with frost across the stiffened ruts of the road, another pleasure is added: for the earth, no longer hidden in her softness, answers with a dim echo, a muffled thud, to every step; so that on a hard road one can play a game clapped in time on the surface of the planet, with astonishment that an object so big and unmanageable as the world rings back to a human foot.

The pleasure of travel is in this answer of the whole earth, potentially, to our steps, so that every good journey must have in it some measure of exploration, and, if possible, an effort of our own. There is no need to go far; a John Gilpin day is enough: imagination only is needed—and an awareness of the horizon rim beyond which the world is new. And if one were asked which, of all the sights in nature, is most lastingly satisfying, would one not choose the horizon?

My father had a theory that, as the child in the womb goes through the various stages of the created animal world,

144

so in early years it continues its progress through the primitive history of man: and it is therefore most necessary, he would say, that children should travel, at the time when in their epitome of history they are nomads by nature.

My sister and I must have gone through a particularly long nomadic age, for we were carried by a guide over the Dolomites in a basket when scarce able to walk, and bundled across the continent incessantly during many following years. My earliest childhood is filled with memories of railway stations arching into darkness, filled with soot and roaring trains, and myself being rushed by some distraught, relentless adult hand—in the days before corridor trains were frequent—to find a lavatory, somewhere. There is a whole series of pictures, seen small as through the wrong end of a telescope, of trains winding into Alpine tunnels, so that one end emerged before the other had gone in; with patches of old snow beside the track, and landscapes far below, elaborate and rocky—streams and cows and châlets—sliding into a peaceful unconscious eternity beneath our comet windows, rattling past.

When the actual joy began I hardly remember: but it was very early. I can recognize the genuine taste of it when I was seven or eight years old, stepping on to an Alpine wayside station in the fresh morning to buy St. Gothard crystals at a booth: the exquisite revelation, a fountain of light within one, that all the world was new. This is only comparable to the ecstasy of love, and less costly and almost equally precious in the end. And there is this about love: that its memory is not enough: for the soul retracts if it does not go on loving, whereas to have travelled once, however long ago—provided it was real and not bogus travel—is enough. It

> would be great impeachment to his age
> In having known no travel in his youth.*

The secret, indeed, is to have it behind you. It is not, like love or education, a process: it is like old china or glass, a collector's object, to acquire and possess.

In one of R. L. Stevenson's most charming stories—*Will*

* SHAKESPEARE. *Two Gentlemen of Verona.*

o' the Mill—the essence of travel is skilfully instilled into a life that never stirs from its own place. The ingredients are there, the imagination is continually busy beyond the visible edge, but it is all seen from his own hill-top, and the hero never strives to turn the intangible into fact. The explanation lies, of course, in the placing of the scene upon a hill: a view is indispensable: there is no travelling without a horizon.

This is, if you come to think of it, just what the bogus traveller lacks. He has made himself a world without a skyline. His rooms are booked in Paris, Cairo, Melbourne, San Francisco, New York: his routes are planned: his days are scheduled: he has blotted out, with every touch of his organization, that blue rim that stands between the known world and the unknown.

For the rest, the chief thing the traveller carries about with him is himself. The places he visits are incidental. He is like the Arab skipper of to-day, or the early trader, steering with carved prow and golden planks well soaked in fish-oil and caulked with bitumen and tow, with sail square to the breeze or slow laborious oars, among the azure-footed islands whose lures and legendary tales are carried to him by tradition and the variable words of men. Islands, sea-changing outlines amethyst or opal, they float to port or starboard, and hold for all a different landfall within their hidden bays. The merchant visits them to unload his own corded bundles upon their sandy beaches, where the moving tide sees to it that every man makes different footprints of his own. There he will unwrap what he has carried, things worked upon and fashioned by the hands and the teaching of his people in his far home and forgotten childhood, the tools and the substance of his journey: and according to the quality of these will entice from their unsuspected places, their sheltered high ravines and wooded coastlands, the strangers whom he seeks. If he has brought with him things rich enough to offer— whose language is universal and whose worth is clear—he may lure his own dreams from their secluded habitations, their unimagined homes, and gain some swift encounter on the sea- beach as he passes, with Circe or Nausicaa as the case may be.

No tickets are needed for these wanderings, and perhaps the fairest journeys have been made by those who never left their houses. Yet the mind needs to be allured, and to dress its thoughts in some shreds of the garment of earth. Our longing to travel is perhaps an admission of insufficiency, a need for stimulus—places, and people, and all the unexpected —for a spur to the mind's journeys. Those large saints in old bad pictures float a very little way above the earth; a landscape is within easy reach below, in case the levitation ceases: and though, to a seer, the whole universe is visible through a needle, most of us like our sight enhanced by novelty or adventure to remember what we see. The small Benvenuto Cellini was slapped by his father when he came upon a salamander in the fire, so that his sensibility, sharpened by surprise, might never forget.

Though it may be unessential to the imagination, travel is necessary to an understanding of men. Only with long experience and the opening of his wares on many a beach where his language is not spoken, will the merchant come to know the worth of what he carries, and what is parochial and what is universal in his choice. Such delicate goods as justice, love and honour, courtesy, and indeed all the things we care for, are valid everywhere; but they are variously moulded and often differently handled, and sometimes nearly unrecognizable if you meet them in a foreign land; and the art of learning fundamental common values is perhaps the greatest gain of travel to those who wish to live at ease among their fellows.

Beyond this and above all is enjoyment with no utilitarian objective, which it is the main business of both travel and education to increase as they can. Good days are to be gathered like sunshine in grapes, to be trodden and bottled into wine and kept for age to sip at ease beside his fire. If the traveller has vintaged well he need trouble to wander no longer; the ruby moments glow in his glass at will. He can still feel the spring in his step, and the wind on his face, though he sit in shelter: unless perhaps the sight of a long road winding, or the singing of the telegraph wires, or the wild duck in their wedges, or horses' hooves that clatter into distance, or the wayside stream—all with their many voices persuade him to try just one more journey before the pleasant world comes to an end.

19

COURAGE

That I may tell pale-hearted fear it lies,
And sleep in spite of thunder.

Macbeth.

Now, if thou be'st that thing divine,
In this day's combat let it shine,
And show that Nature wants an art
To conquer one resolvèd heart.

MARVELL. *A Dialogue between the Resolved Soul and Created Pleasure.*

He all their ammunition
And feats of war defeats,
With plain heroic magnitude of mind.

MILTON. *Samson Agonistes.*

I will show you fear in a handful of dust.

T. S. ELIOT. *The Waste Land.*

. . . and sweet,
O love, to lay down fear at love's fair feet;

SWINBURNE. *Erotion.*

To speak of it (valour) in it selfe, It is a quality which he
that hath, shall have least need of:

DONNE. *An Essay of Valour.*

While loud and louder thro' the dazed head of the
SPHINX
the old lion's voice roareth o'er all the lands.

ROBERT BRIDGES. *Testament of Beauty*, I, 789.

I have almost forgot the taste of fears.

Macbeth.

19. COURAGE

ENGLISH education has concentrated on withstanding fear. We were brought up on this principle, and it seems to me as I look back to have been the first and most important thing we learnt. Parents who picked us off the ground when we tumbled appeared anxious, not to find out our hurts, but to keep us from crying. That cliché about the "stiff upper lip," which desperately quivered into sobs, must surely come from childhood. At six years old we were put on to ponies, and at seven allowed to believe that we hunted, in small red coats whose woolly brilliance I can still think of with delight. I see now how much of pride came into courage, instilled drop by drop from a grown-up world where Fear was apparently unknown! Pride when one did not cry and was allowed for the whole day to be called *Joan*, in memory of Joan of Arc, who—to me at the age of six— was the favourite heroine. And there was terrible humiliation when the ideal was not sustained. I was never, I believe, really free from fear on horseback like my sister, who made for anything without a thought. There was at the bottom of my heart a little black pool into which I dared not look; and this, in moments of agony, before a jump or a yawning peat-bog, such as crowded our high moors, would suddenly enlarge itself and fill me not only with fear itself, but with the sordid shame of being afraid. How deeply this inhibition must have penetrated my unconscious memory I only discovered a few years ago when, extremely tired in the middle of the war, I spent a summer writing a book at the house of friends near my old home on Dartmoor. The whole region had been taken over for the training of American troops,

who certainly carried away a grim picture of the English
countryside; for few places can be more desolate than the
moors where the five rivers rise, oozing out of a central high
cushion-land of bog, reddish in colour, blackly seamed with
cracks, and very like a desert that is soft. A few "cuts," as
they are called, have been made for those who can find them.
Here a horse may walk on the granite floor, while the peat
walls rise on either side soft as chocolate, higher than horse's
head and rider's. When the mist spins and the south-west
wind bends the heavy-headed grasses, and the heather sings
like telegraph wires near the ground, the whole landscape
turns swiftly into a Mother of Streams; waters pour down
rejected by the saturated earth, and the rivers spread fans of
yellow foam over their boulders. But on fine days there is a
wrinkled beauty in the solitude. One can find a way into
it on foot, avoiding the treacherous patches red or green,
jumping from tussock to tussock, judging one's distance and
knowing that one is safe where heather grows. The easy
slopes close like shutting doors as one enters a landscape
where even the wild ponies dare not come. Here, between
soft banks in mild rushy hollows where not a stone is seen,
the new-born rivers—Dart, Teign, Okement or Tavy—lie still
and dark as amber.

I used to know this country well enough and, when I
returned after so many years, at once borrowed a pony; but
I had forgotten some of the bad places, and soon found myself
among eye-holes of bog on a hillside and, trusting to the little
mare's sagacity, laid the reins on her neck to let her find her
way. A moorland pony will usually avoid bog at all costs,
but this one had evidently been corrupted by stables and
civilization, and walked straight in. I slipped off, while
she floundered wildly, and lifted herself out with her hoof on
my shinbone, which was also submerged. We turned home in
a sober mood, and it was some weeks before I could ride again.
When I did so I was visited by Fear: all the fears, perhaps, of
my childhood gathered into one. The summer days spread
a robe of quiet over the wild places: the Americans and their
guns, thudding and shuddering into the yielding hills, were
audible but invisible: the danger of their bombardment
had emptied even the last few isolated farms that lie with tiny

walled patches of field adrift on the desolation of the moors. I rode daily into this solitude, skirting the bogs from afar, with a feeling of horror as I approached them; until, at a hundred yards or so, quite secure from any possibility of harm, I found I could go on no longer; my whole being transformed itself into a sort of negation; and—wondering at the strangeness of it—I would turn away sooner or later, exhausted, towards the high safe ground.

Civilizations do not degenerate through fear, but because they forget that Fear exists: it is easy to lose the knowledge of the waste land through which our sources ooze into the light. In that foreland are Hunger and Love, the oldest of all passions. They lie dormant even in roots and fronds of vegetable forms before animals appear: they show themselves against the first mineral background, alive and inexplicable as twisted pines that suck their nourishment out of nakedness, hanging upon a rock. Into their simple world consciousness comes, and with it Fear is born. And Fear and Love and Hunger still stride about us, dark-eyed with chaos, wearing our clothes uneasily. They are the three figures of the world's drama that move immense and regardless on the stage among the ant-heaps of men, like those Egyptian kings on a frieze, with spears uplifted. And they hold all other passions in their hand, such as pride and anger, which are but satellites of Fear.

Hunger and Love are favourable to life though surrounded by ruthlessness and danger, and therefore there is a human loyalty towards them. But with fear there is no truce. No taming, no hedge, no direction, can make his way other than an evil way for men: he has no footprint that is not calamity: and all the triumph of a human life is bound to his defeat.

Therefore we exalt valour above all virtues, because by it we hope to be liberated from this most deadly, ancient and universal of all our adversaries; and with valour alone for a weapon, and Love and Hunger on our side, have fought through the aeons of our history, a long battle with few victories and many defeats. Few as they are, they are acclaimed with so universal a consent, with so personal a rejoicing, that it is evidently clear to us how every defeat of Fear is gain for all.

There is, therefore, much to be said for the English teaching, which makes the whole aim of life a resistance to Fear. Even our smallest habits, our cultivation of discomforts, our walking in all weathers and bathing in cold water, our difficult spelling and monstrous weights and measures, our draughty houses and rigorous cooking—are all a part of the training to endure. And not in physical things only, but in the disciplines of restraint and silence, of modesty and the toleration of others, there is a protection of one's identity under attack as it were, a strengthening of the passive forms of courage, and a clearing of the ground where it may grow: so that by specializing so much in resistance we have become tough and quiet, courageous but not militant, with a valour devoted to combat fear and not to create it: and we are, I believe, as a nation easier than most to live with in this world.

Yet it would be a mistake to think that victory comes by these methods and no others. Our road is a good road; but the main highway has a signpost that says: "Perfect love casteth out fear." This is something more positive than resistance, a warmth where all resistance melts. It explains the courage of the saints, who alone can forget Fear with impunity. And a fundamental difference between nations —between the Italians and English, for instance—lies in their choice, however imperfectly applied, of one or the other of these thoroughfares.

There is certainly no toughening of the Italian child. If he falls, the whole family rushes to the rescue: he sets up his howl with a secure and comfortable feeling that all the world is ready to attend. And so he goes on through life. Women are different, they are toughened everywhere by the nature of things, since they cannot even bear children without facing the darkness of eternity: but the men in Italy go wrapped in a cocoon of domestic affection from the arms of their mothers to those of their mistresses or wives (or usually both) until in their turn they pour this same familiar gentleness over their yearly babies as they come. Not until the deeply-rooted habit of affection is touched does the Italian develop what we call courage—a resistance to fear: when he does so, it is based entirely on human relationships, and will never make an army of soldiers. But it explains why thousands of our prisoners (or German or Russian prisoners, or anyone, for that matter, I believe), could walk from village to village and find help and food and sympathy and hiding, whatever the danger that attended them.

It also explains the astonishing transformation that is wrought in such a country by the infliction of cruelty, which in a short time turns indifference into a resistance so general as to become unquenchable, being based not upon personal strength but upon Love. This ancient ally will fight against Fear when called upon to do so, and stands beside men in their need.

It is easy for us on the whole to understand a people like the Arabs, I think, because their code of resistance is much the same as ours. But if with the Latin nations we are generally perplexed and nearly always wrong, it is chiefly because we call things by different names, and because their courage and our courage are not the same. It takes many years of friendship and understanding to realize that they are devoted as we are to the combating and not the creating of Fear, and that we are engaged by different, almost opposite, methods in a common warfare against the oldest and perhaps the only enemy of man.

20

OLD AGE

Dans ce trajet si court de la branche à la terre,
Comme elles savent mettre une beauté dernière,
Et malgré leur terreur de pourrir sur le sol,
Veulent que cette chute ait la grâce d'un vol!

           E. ROSTAND.   *Cyrano de Bergerac.*

        Failing, yet gracious,
        Slow pacing, soon homing.
        A patriarch that strolls
        Through the tents of his children.

         WILLIAM HENLEY.   *Rhymes and Rhythms.*

'Twas at that hour of beauty when the setting sun
squandereth his cloudy bed with rosy hues, to flood
his lov'd works as in turn he biddeth them Good-night;
and all the towers and temples and mansions of men
face him in bright farewell,

        ROBERT BRIDGES.   *Testament of Beauty*, IV, 1268.

Burn now your candle as long as ye will: it has naught to
do with me, for my light cometh when the day breaketh.

             THE VENERABLE BEDE.

      I joy, that in these straits I see my west;

        DONNE.   *Hymn to God My God, in my Sickness.*

      If Light can thus deceive, wherefore not Life?

           JOSEPH BLANCO WHITE.

      And like a new-born spirit did he pass
      Through the green evening quiet in the sun,

           KEATS.   *Endymion*, II.

20. OLD AGE

TEETOTALLERS, as they grow old, must look back with sadness at the shores of their life strewn with refusals—dull little wrecks, split on no reef of circumstance, but bogged and abandoned as it were in weeds. The real teetotaller cannot limit only alcohol. Most things, if he comes to think about them, are harmful in excess: food, and the more transitory ways of love; and Tolstoy added music. Some men might put clothes, some women golf and fishing.

> While Adam in his garden spent
> His hours in a calm content
> His lady engineered his fall:
> She *was* so tired of it all.

It is a sobering, or inebriating, thought that a purist teetotal wife might conceivably prohibit gardening. Gambling, racing, betting, are doomed—and the Stock Exchange too. And one cannot logically prohibit drugs and read the Sunday press. There is no end to it. A Father of the Church has said that "even of sitting, as of all carnal pleasures, there cometh satiety."

But a sound instinct in human beings will not respect virtues that are compelled. One of the few advantages of riches is that they make austerities voluntary; and teetotalism strikes directly at this freedom. It strikes at the very keystone of liberty, the principle of freewill itself. It interposes its puny rigid NO between man and the elasticity of choice, allowed by the Gods for all occasions. And what principle underlies this impertinence? A mere squalor that holds moderation impossible, and places safety in impotence alone.

159

Are we able to divorce? We will be unfaithful in love. Are we strong? We will certainly go to war. We sip our glass? We shall overdrink to drunkenness. And now, with governments planning right and left, our ability even to walk about the world and to earn our living and direct our labour is being doubted and fenced in more and more: so that it looks as if we were soon to be teetotal all over.

If this is so, there will be fewer happy old men left as the years pass, for the contentment of age depends upon a not too abstemious youth. Minds are kept active with enjoyment and there is no reason not to like one thing because one likes another, when there is room for so many. This is why much is forgiven to polygamists and amateurs: while even the specialist monogamist is only a man who discovers the intrinsic variety of the one. As we follow animals from molluscs or earthworms to man, we see, emerging slowly,

A speck, a mist, a shape——

the figure of Boredom. It is noticeable in dogs, cats and horses, and I am convinced that wild animals die of it in captivity. In human beings it is perhaps the goad to civilization, pricking the slow team to jolt along: and if men, as they say, invent so many more things than women, this is probably merely due to the fact that they often sit about in the house with nothing particular to do.

Moderation must never be pursued like art for art's sake only; but should be pressed out of the fullness of life as a drop that has to unite many savours, so that only a little of each can be afforded in our span of time. There are factories for vermouth on the plain of Piedmont, whose mountain scent is wafted across country as one drives. There, beside the sheds and high chimneys, strips are laid out and planted with gentian and thyme, and grey-leaved wormwood that gives the vermouth its name, and many other aromatic herbs brought down from the pastoral high valleys: so that when a glass is offered, it holds in its few mouthfuls the whole taste, sweet and bitter, of the hills. Such is life, and the art of it is to judge the mixture of the flavours, so that your vermouth, far from being reprehensible, may do what it is intended to do, and give you *an appetite for more.*

Old age, after well-filled days, learns to distil these substances and test their permanent values, and enters a timeless world where years need scarcely count.   There it can avoid such aversion as meets old people who cling to inconstant things, even in slight matters—even in amusement, or in dress.   For the shams that youth may wear lose their illusion: lace, silks and jewels must acquire a durable beauty to be tolerable; and any extreme of temporary fashion comes to jar.   In personal relations, change must be held no longer clasped and rebellious in its brief prison of the will, but left to ebb and flow, while its unchanging background counts more and more.   Failure to attend to these things is, I think, the whole reason for the misunderstanding, so very common in England, between age and youth.   Old men retired find the centre of their being in committees still: and women cling to their haunts with haggard looks, like climbers on an ice slope whose feet have slipped, who drag, on the sliding brightness, at those to whom their weight is tied: youth looks upon them as enemies, since they encumber his ways.   "Besides, Sir, there must always be a struggle between a father and son, while one aims at power and the other at independence."*

I have often fancied how, if I were a man burdened with a career, I should like to be made a consul or vice-consul in a small and unimportant place of my own choosing, with a guarantee that no promotion need ever come my way; so that I might grow into it and love it at leisure, and forget to look at the advancements of others, nor feel their eyes upon my own.   There, I believe, knowing one divorced from any thought of power, young men and women would come gladly for advice, safe in the knowledge that the *doing* still rested in their hands.   But the fact is that we are a people teetotal about thinking, whatever we may be about drink: and the idea of leisure in obscurity, with *thought* for enjoyment, makes no very general appeal.

It comes more easily in other lands.

I happened one evening long ago to reach Banias, where the river Jordan rises under the shrine of Pan.   The Crusader castle of Montfort lies extended upon the height above, and foothills crowd around it and rise with the whole sweep of

* JAMES BOSWELL. *Life of Samuel Johnson.*

northern Palestine towards the majesty of Hermon. I was visiting this castle but had been caught by the late afternoon; so I enquired my way and spent the night in the house of the Sheikh of Banias, in a room with nine uncurtained windows and a bed of hard bolsters and yellow satin quilts. The Sheikh had never received a European before, nor did he ask even my name, but with their general courtesy prepared the best he had and entertained me, and sent me with a guide next morning: and when I returned, took me up steps to where his mother lived on the top story of the house, in two rooms with a terrace filled with pots of flowers.

This beautiful old lady was dressed in white, and her face was framed in the high white coif of the Druses, to whom she belonged. When we had talked a while, she put her hand on my arm and took me to a balcony. It hung out over space where the land fell away from what had once been the city wall. The Jordan danced below, invisible beneath a fluttering carpet made by the tops of poplar trees, through which the gay voice of the stream came singing. The white and green leaves played like shot silk in the wind. And beyond their restless delight the marshland of Hule stretched with black cattle grazing, and wattle huts, and reeds. Beyond it again were the highlands of Safed.

"I have been here thirty years," the old lady said.

I asked her if she ever left Banias, or even the house she lived in.

"Never," she said.

"Do you find time heavy on your hands?"

"No," she said. "When my eyes are tired, I open this window and watch the sea-wind moving in the trees. And when my heart is tired, I sit alone and think of God."

The West can find small solace in quite such quietude, and there is justification, after all, for gaiety in age. For the joy of youth is the setting out on its voyage, but the happiness of age has achievement behind it and a landfall in sight; it is no small thing to come without shipwreck within hail of one's anchorage: and if one is able still to take pleasure in things that pleased at the starting, in strength and agility of body or elegance of dress, or rapier-play of talk—why, it is so much added, a last sweet-meat thrown to tilt the measure of life in our favour a little beyond the weight we could expect; it is an innocent delight that few will grudge us, if we carry it on the circumference and not in the centre of our mind.

On the whole, age comes most gently to those who have some doorway into an abstract world,—art, or philosophy, or learning—regions where the years are scarcely noticed and young and old can meet in a pale truthful light. We move there with increasing freedom as Time rubs out the illusions of possession, whose dark attendant, envy, fades away. The loss of our own things, or such we thought so, our faculties, our friends, our loves—makes us again receptive as in childhood, though now it is no human hand that gives. In our increasing poverty, the universal riches grow more apparent, the careless showering of gifts regardless of return; our private grasp lessens, and leaves us heirs to infinite loves in a common world where every joy is a part of one's personal joy. With a loosening hold returning towards acceptance, we prepare in the anteroom for a darkness where even this last personal flicker fades, and what happens will be in the Giver's hand alone.

The shared universe, the escape from their own individual cell, gives to the eyes of some old men and women a clear and happy look, a delight for all who follow them to see. It is perhaps more frequent among labouring people, or in countries where the old are accustomed to live with their children and children's children, as is general all about the Mediterranean. This greater happiness does not, I think, come from a greater measure of youth preserved by living with the young: for who does not know the dim old Latin ladies who live among their grand-children and nieces, with an outline long since blurred in black, and faded from its original contour, negations as it were personified? This very loss of outline makes them happy; it is a liberation from the regards of others, a merging into the current of other lives, a finding of that self which youth with its hedge of beauty and maturity with its eyes on the target have made unreal for years. By these they were shut away from their right estate, which is nothing less than all the world of men: and the light in the eyes of old age is that of an opening door. One sees it too in old countrymen and sailors, who also merge and forget themselves in a universal world.

I have had the good fortune to know and love a number of such old people, and dearest perhaps of all was my godfather, W. P. Ker. He joined us every year in the Alps to climb, and would say that, if released blindfold on a mountain top, he could open his eyes and know whether he stood north or south of the Italian border: the Swiss and Italian valleys are cut in different shapes. He carried Dante or Pindar in his pocket, and walked with the slow mountain step that scarcely knows a difference in age or youth. In rust-coloured tweeds with a knapsack, however small the journey, and a battered old hat which he swept off and held in his hand when he stood on a pass with a view, he would walk in a companionable silence, with the world and its histories moving easily in and out of his thoughts. His silence, and immense learning, made one shy—as if one were offering crumbs to an elephant. On the day when I first climbed on a rope, as we came down through the summer pastures to little streams that drum and tunnel under banks of turf—he suddenly left his path and stepped ankle-deep into the water, and came back to me saying: "I always like to do it with my boots on, because they never let me as a boy."

On his last climb, when he was seventy, two other goddaughters and a guide were with us, and we set out for a spur of Monte Rosa through meadows underneath the later stars. When the dawn hit the snows with red spears we reached a high scooped corrie, still cold and unawakened from the night, where the grasses end beside a fanlike stream. Here we drank and rested, and watched the gaiety of day spilling from its high cup; and on the mountain-side an hour or so above, on stony slabs so steep that I had to cut him a resting-place with my ice-axe, he suddenly gave a small cry and died. Our guide went with one girl to the valley for help, while two remained. The place was high and steep. Only space surrounded it, and rock and snows beyond. Soon white mists came browsing like cold flocks and hid the habitable world. We sat waiting there for seven hours, watching the changes of death. His face, so dear, lost all the mortal lines of age; every hour as it passed brought a new shield of

peace. It was not youth that returned, but a beauty neither
of life nor time, and yet himself, as we had divined him but
never seen beneath the little waves of living. The features,
so familiar, and majestic now, seemed in their estranged
borderland of mortality to be one with the mountains about
us, in that place where the oldest laws of earth and the most
enduring are listened to alone. Men came from the village
and laid him, wrapped in a blanket, on a ladder, and carried
him down across the snow; and we followed him with pacified
quiet hearts, as if we had seen no sudden interruption, but
one who in his progress reached a porch and stayed a while
with the inner majesty of the temple already upon him,
before he went on his way.

My soul stands
Now past the midway from mortality,
And so I can prepare without a sigh
To tell thee briefly all my joy and pain.

KEATS. *Endymion, III.*

Souvienne-vous de celuy à qui, comme on demanda
à quoy faire il se peinoit si fort en un art qui ne pouvoit
venir à la cognoissance de guères de gents : "J'en ay assez
de peu," respondit il; "j'en ay assez d'un; j'en ay assez de
pas un."

MONTAIGNE. *Essays.*

EPILOGUE

IT is February, and raining—a cold spring rain. In the
Dolomites, behind mists and foothills, this rain is snow;
the hesitating flakes, whiter than the sky that produces
them, are falling on uninhabited places, or on pastures only
visited in summer; they press, like the lives of men, thick
and gentle, out of a blankness teeming with their numbers,
and cover each other with oblivion. If they make a sound
at all, it is some tiny crackle of crystal layers, imperceptible
as our world's noises to a star. They have no memory of the
clouds and dews and the sources from which they come.
They are wound into the stuff of the world, and their familiar
outline is sharp only because darkness surrounds it, as the
harmony of words or music flowers out of silence.

Across the slanting lattice of the rain I can see a few of
the thirteen roads and paths that wind from various places
to our city on the hill. They show brown already, and make
the pockets and grass-flattened slopes and rises upholding
them look green in spite of winter bareness; and the naked
outlines of trees if you look closely have a premonition of
life, a scarce visible promise along the smaller boughs where
buds will break. The roads wind in the deserted landscape.
They descend from where every bend and coppice is known
to me since childhood, into the plain which now looks like
a slate that is being sponged over, under whose sodden mists
the cities of Vicenza, Padua and Venice lie equidistant, heal-
ing themselves of war. The roads become invisible, but I can
follow them through the land I know, the chess-board of the
plain dotted with pawns of houses, and palaces and cathedrals
here and there, and small towns—Cittadella, Castelfranco,

Bassano—whose defensive walls now make a background for pedlars' booths on market days. Into the roads a thousand lateral lanes come like tributaries, winding their ancient way round boundaries of maize and corn and clover, with ditches choked with yellow water-flags in spring or tunnelled with leaves in summer. The great roads cut straight, and the small ones, gradual out of the soil, waste time and length in their respect of landmarks; progress and tradition are embodied in the contrast. But whether old or new, they all go on, with feet or wheels upon them, beyond Padua and Vicenza and the familiar towns, till they turn with the roundness of the world; and the rays from the eyes of those who walk upon them pierce the universe at an angle different from ours.

It is lucky to live in a city on a hill and to be saved by the view at one's window from thinking of the world as flat, so that one may see at a glance how all we have in sight slips over some edge into the veils of space. It makes the notice in London taxicabs, that the "fare is inclusive of time and distance," sound arrogant. Nothing that we can reach is inclusive of time and distance. And as I am here, returned from the war to a house still standing, I think that my life too stands clear and sharp, its watershed just behind it, and the footsteps that led to its present moment fair and familiar in the remembered morning. Before it are the afternoon slopes, gentler—one hopes—and bathed in that mellowness which seems to be the contribution of earth to the swordlike brilliance of the planets. In it the dust and smoke of labours catch the sun; the steam of tillage attracts the dews; it is the habitable atmosphere of men. And this path too, long or short, when its "sun hath stretched out all the hills," will lead across the circumference of the world and glimmer of evening to the nocturnal folds.

This is the prospect from the watershed, and when the traveller reaches it, it is a good thing to take an hour's leisure and look out on the visible portions of the journey, since never in one's life can one see the same view twice. I have placed my bundle beside me and found a flat stone and settled in the sun with my back to the road of my coming, and have looked as far as I can into the valley where the track is lost. And as the eye soon tires with so little detail to hold

it, and the mist wreathes all in its timeless festoons, and
no mortal inn is in sight—I have opened my bundle and
sorted the few things collected and carried through the
morning's climb, to count what personal oddments are there
to help me on my way. This little book is the list of these
things; and as it is a random assortment, not harvested from
learning but from life and accident, it is probably just like
the list of millions of other travellers, since the journey we
make is the same. Who asks for originality in a soldier's
kit-bag, or the knapsack of a mountaineer? Or who would
not think it presumptuous in the snowflake to wish to be
unique in its manner of falling to the ground? My hope is
the very opposite; for we are all—unless suddenly cut off—
bound to grow old; and as I am fortunate in looking to old
age without either misgiving or regret, but with an interest of
travel—I like to think that these stray reflections may not
have been written for myself only, but for all who have
climbed and crossed their ridges and are standing with me
upon the verge of afternoon.

ASOLO, 1948.

PERSEUS IN THE WIND

Dame Freya Stark was born in Paris on 31 January 1893. Her first journey was to the Middle East in 1928, her latest to Nepal in 1981. By her vivid accounts of travel in Persia, Arabia and the Near East, her many readers have themselves become travellers at heart.

When not travelling, Dame Freya lives in Asolo, Italy, where she was brought up. She ascribes her great love of adventure partly to early training in the Dolomites with her parents, who would trek from Asolo across the Pelmo Pass to Cortina, where they caught the train to London. At the age of two, in their trip of 1895, Freya Stark was already showing an extraordinary degree of independence, constantly straying away from her parents, off the beaten track. That independence has been the secret of her success as a traveller and a writer. *Perseus in the Wind* is a personal and individual kind of book and deals with a different kind of journey to that described in her travel memoirs. It is a reflective journey in which Freya Stark has 'written about things that are beyond our grasp yet visible to all, dear to our hearts and far from our understanding as the constellations; a comfort for the frail light they shed'. It is an inspiring and stimulating book written from the heart of one of this country's great travellers and writers.